The Ultimate
Moroccan Cookbook

111 Dishes From Morocco To Cook Right Now

Slavka Bodic

Imprint: Independently published

Please sign up for free Balkan and Mediterranean recipes:
www.balkanfood.org

Introduction

Moroccan cuisine has been highly acclaimed over time for its pleasing, tempting, and irresistible tastes and aromas. In sum, Morocco's unique culinary culture has gained many influences from all over Africa, the Middle East, and Europe, and those diverse and delectable traits are reflected through the diversity of flavors that in the amazing array Moroccan entrees, desserts, drinks, breakfasts, etc. The great benefit about Moroccan food is that it isn't only tasty, but it's also rich in healthy and nutritious ingredients. It offers your number of Mediterranean fruits, vegetables, tropical fruits, grains, beans, legumes, seafood, meats, etc. So if you're curious about Moroccan Cuisine and want to explore all its fabulous flavors, then this cookbook offers the perfect read for you!

As a result, *The 111 Moroccan Recipes Cookbook* will introduce to the Moroccan cuisine and its culinary culture in a way that you've never experienced before. It delivers a variety of Moroccan recipes in one place. The book is great for all those who are keen to cook healthy food and want to explore its unique flavors. With the help of this Moroccan cuisine cookbook, you can create a complete Moroccan menu at home, or you can try all the special Moroccan recipes for your special occasions and celebrations. In this cookbook, you'll find popular Moroccan meals and the ones that you might not have heard of. From nourishing breakfasts to all of the vegetable soups, the exotic desserts, drinks, main dishes, and Moroccan salads, etc., you'll sample them all. And all these recipes are created in such a simple way that those who aren't even familiar with the Moroccan culture, food, and language can still try and cook them at home without facing much difficulty.

Moroccan culinary culture and cuisine are full of surprises. You'd never expect to have a mix of Western and Eastern cuisines all in one place, but Moroccan food makes that possible with its Spanish and middle eastern influences. And if you want to bring all those flavors to your dinner table, then give this book a thorough read to discover all the answers in one place.

What you can find in this Cookbook:
- Overview about the Moroccan Cuisine
- Insights About Morocco
- Moroccan Breakfast Recipes
- Snacks, Sides, or Appetizers
- Soup Recipes
- Main Dishes and Entrees
- Moroccan desserts
- And Moroccan Drinks....

Let's try all these Moroccan Recipes and recreate a complete menu to celebrate the amazing Moroccan flavors and tantalizing aromas!

Why Moroccan Cuisine?

Moroccan cuisine is deeply influenced and heavily inspired by the country's exchanges and interactions with other nations and cultures throughout history. Moroccan cuisine is a combination of Arab, Amazigh, Mediterranean, and Andalusian cuisines, with slight influences from Europe, especially French, Spanish, and sub-Saharan cuisines.

Morocco is a country that produces a variety of Mediterranean and tropical vegetables and exotic fruits. Meats like a goat, beef, mutton, chicken, lamb, and seafood, are mostly used in this cuisine.

Popular flavorings include:
- *Lemon pickle*
- *Argan oil*
- *Unrefined olive oil*
- *Dried fruits*

Being heavily influenced by Mediterranean cuisine, the Moroccan diet further emphasizes the use of wheat, couscous, and olive oil as a staple food. Grapes and wine are also used staples in the country.

Spices are used extensively in Moroccan cuisine. Saffron, mint, olives, and Talaouine, from Meknes, and oranges and lemons are home- produced and are being exported from the country. Commonly used Moroccan spices include turmeric, cumin, ginger, cinnamon, coriander, paprika, saffron, cloves, mace, fennel, nutmeg, anise, cayenne pepper, fenugreek, caraway, black pepper, and sesame seeds. 27 of these spices are combined to make a Moroccan spice mixture called ras el hanout. Herbs that are commonly used in Moroccan cuisine include:

- *Mint*
- *Parsley*
- *Coriander*
- *Oregano*
- *Peppermint*
- *Marjoram*
- *Verbena*
- *Sage*

Famous Moroccan recipes that you must try on this cuisine include:

- **Chebakia:** It's a traditional Moroccan dessert made from rolled dough roses, served with sweet syrup and sesame seeds.
- **Kaab al ghazal:** Also known as gazelle horns, the Kaab al ghazal are stuffed curled cookies that are stuffed and fried.
- **Harira:** It's a traditional Moroccan soup that is now cooked in different varieties. It has a mix of different veggies, beans, and meat.
- **Tagine:** You'll find different varieties of tagine from fish, poultry, and vegetable tagine.

Morocco

If you search for Morocco on the world map, you'll find the country on the north-west corner of the African continent, and the country serves as the closest link between Europe and African continents. For this reason, it remained the center of several civilizations. In each era, it was inhabited by major world civilization, and today you can see the influences of the history within the current Moroccan culture and culinary traditions. The Kingdom of Morocco is located in North Africa, and its coastline touches the Mediterranean Sea. Its land borders connect it to the Western Sahara and Algeria.

The area that we now know as Morocco has been inhabited by different civilizations since the Paleolithic era, from 190,000 to 90,000 BC. Recent research demonstrated that it had been populated by people for 315,000 years. This region was more fertile in the early ages than today, because it had a savanna landscape back then. In contrast, its landscape today is arid. Twenty-two thousand years ago, Iberomaurusian culture was taken over by the Aterian culture. The place also remained the hub for several Muslim and non-Muslim dynasties, and you can see those elements within the great architecture and old heritage preserved in different parts of the country.

The Badii Palace, located in Marrakesh in the old citadel, was built during the Almohad Dynasty. The palace is worth visiting if you want to go back in time and learn more about history. Morocco had also attracted French and Spanish invaders; and every time they invaded the place, they left their influences on the country, its people, language, and culture, which are still quite visible today. And that's what I personally loved about this country: it has so much to offer, and you can spend months going from places to places, but the place is so full of surprises and its gorgeous architecture will leave you spellbound.

My knowledge of Morocco and Moroccan cuisine is widely sourced from a friend of mine with whom I traveled to the country a few years back. Though my stay in the country was for a few days, it was magical. My Moroccan friend taught me so much about the Moroccan people and culture in such a short duration. While I was there, I stayed in Rabat, the capital, and visited several restaurants. I personally met all the chefs working there and collected information about their specialties and what makes the Moroccan cuisine so special. This cookbook is greatly inspired by my last visit to Morocco, and most of the recipes that I've shared here are motivated by, sourced, and learned from native Moroccans. Needless to say, people there were extremely helping and welcoming, and I loved spending time with them while learning and experimenting with the traditional Moroccan recipes.

Table of Contents

ONE LAST THING 170

Breakfast

Sfenj

Preparation time: 15 minutes
Cook time: 15 minutes
Nutrition facts (per serving): 169 cal (5.3g fat, 4g protein, 0g fiber)

This *Sfenj* is one healthy breakfast that can be served with powdered sugar toppings and is functions as the Moroccan morning doughnut.

Ingredients (6 servings)
2 teaspoons yeast
1 1/4 cups warm water
3 cups all-purpose flour
1 teaspoon salt
Vegetable oil for frying
Granulated sugar or powdered sugar

Preparation
Mix yeast with warm water in a suitable bowl and leave it for 15 minutes. Mix flour, salt, and yeast water in a bowl until it makes a sticky dough. Cover this bowl with a kitchen towel and leave it for 4 hours. Fill a deep pot with vegetable oil up to 3 inches and heat over a medium flame. Divide the dough into plum-sized balls, and deep fry them until golden brown. Then transfer to a plate with a slotted spoon. Dust these balls with sugar and serve.

Msemen

Preparation time: 15 minutes
Cook time: 15 minutes
Nutrition facts (per serving): 256 cal (5.2g fat, 3g protein, 18g fiber)

Have you tried *Msema* for breakfast? Well, here's a Moroccan delight that adds semolina and white flour to your morning meal in a delicious way.

Ingredients (4 servings)
3 1/2 cups white flour
1/2 cup fine semolina
2 teaspoon sugar
2 teaspoon salt
1/4 teaspoon dry yeast
1 1/2 cups warm water

For Folding
1 cup of vegetable oil
1/2 cup fine semolina
1/4 cup unsalted butter

Preparation
Mix white flour with semolina, sugar, salt, yeast, warm water in a mixing bowl until it makes a smooth dough. Divide the dough into small plum-sized balls, roll them and place them in a greased tray. Cover these balls with a plastic wrap and leave for 15 minutes. Grease your working surface and hands with cooking oil. Dip one dough ball in the oil and then spread it in a rough circle. Add a dot of butter on top and drizzle semolina on top. Fold the dough into a rectangle, add a dot of butter, drizzle of semolina again, and fold it into a square. Repeat the same steps with the remaining balls. Place a suitable griddle over medium heat. Spread one square of the dough into a 1/8-inch-thick sheet and cook it in the griddle for almost 3 minutes per side until golden. Serve.

Baghrir

Preparation time: 10 minutes
Cook time: 12 minutes
Nutrition facts (per serving): 219 cal (12g fat, 2g protein, 10g fiber)

Best to serve at breakfast, *Baghrir* is great as an energizing breakfast. It's a Moroccan version of fluffy morning pancakes.

Ingredients (6 servings)
2 1/2 cups warm water
1/2 tablespoon dry yeast
1 cup semolina
1/2 cup all-purpose flour
A dash of salt
1/2 tablespoon baking powder

Preparation
Blend warm water, yeast, flour, semolina, flour, baking powder, and salt in a blender. Transfer the dough to a suitable container then cover it and leave for 30 minutes. Place an 8 inches skillet over medium heat and pour ½ cup semolina batter into the skillet and cook for 2 minutes per side. Make more pancakes using the remaining batter. Serve.

Moroccan Harcha Flatbread

Preparation time: 15 minutes
Cook time: 20 minutes
Nutrition facts (per serving): 213 cal (10g fat, 9g protein, 7g fiber)

The *Moroccan Harcha flatbread* is famous for its delicious flavor and crumbly texture. Made out of semolina, this flatbread goes well with all types of egg omelets.

Ingredients (16 servings)
2 cups (350 grams) fine semolina
3 tablespoons sugar
2 teaspoons baking powder
1/4 teaspoon salt
1/2 cup (125 grams) soft butter
3/4 cup (180 ml) milk
1/4 cup coarse semolina

Preparation
Blend semolina, sugar, salt, baking powder, and butter in a blender. Pour in the milk and mix until it makes a dough. Leave the dough for 15 minutes. During this time, place a griddle over medium-low heat. Divide the dough into balls of the desired size. Flatten each ball into ¼ inch thick round. Cook the *Harcha* for 5 to 10 minutes per side on low heat until golden brown. Serve warm.

Pistachio Briouates

Preparation time: 15 minutes
Cook time: 12 minutes
Nutrition facts (per serving): 256 cal (16gfat, 9g protein, 6g fiber)

Pistachio Briouates are another nutritious yet simple meal for the breakfast table. They offer lots of nuts and pastry sheets, which are cooked together in a tempting combination.

Ingredients (12 servings)
5 ounces (150 grams) blanched hazelnuts
5 ounces (150 grams) unsalted shelled pistachios
3 ounces (80 grams) caster sugar
3 tablespoons orange blossom water, divided
½ teaspoon ground cinnamon
½ teaspoon ground dried ginger
1 teaspoon salt
2 tablespoons (30 grams) unsalted butter, softened
1/2 tablespoon (20 grams) unsalted butter melted
7 1/2 ounces (200 grams) filo pastry
10 1/2 ounces (300 grams) honey
Groundnuts or chopped dried fruits for decoration

Preparation
At 350 degrees F, preheat your oven. Roast the hazelnuts in a baking tray by baking in the oven. Transfer the nuts to a food processor. Add pistachios, 2 tablespoons orange blossom water, salt, ginger, cinnamon, and caster sugar before processing process into a paste. Transfer the pistachio mixture to a bowl, add butter, and then mix well. Spread and cut the filo sheet in 3x12 inch rectangles. Cover the rectangles with a damp towel. Place one filo rectangle on a working surface and brush its top with butter. Add pistachio paste at the top corner of the rectangle then fold it into a triangle to make *Briouates*. Repeat the

same steps with the remaining rectangles. Place the triangles in a baking tray and brush them with melted butter and bake for 12 minutes until golden brown. Meanwhile, mix honey and 1 tablespoon orange blossom water in a cooking pan and heat this mixture. Dip the baked *Briouates* in the honey mixture for 2 minutes. Remove from the liquid and garnish with nuts. Serve.

Chebakia

Preparation time: 15 minutes
Cook time: 10 minutes
Nutrition facts (per serving): 232 cal (4g fat, 5g protein, 1.4g fiber)

Try this *Moroccan Chebakia* for your breakfast or dessert, and you'll forget about the rest. The recipe is simple and gives you lots of nutrients in one place.

Ingredients (8 servings)
Chebakia
1 teaspoon dry active yeast
½ teaspoon caster sugar
17 1/2 ounces (500 grams) plain flour
9 ounces (250 grams) sesame seeds, ground
9 ounces (250 grams) almond flour
1 large egg
¼ cup white vinegar
¼ cup orange blossom water
1/4 cup (80 ml) melted butter
1/4 cup (80 ml) cup olive oil
¼ teaspoon ground turmeric
½ teaspoon ground cinnamon
½ teaspoon ground anise
Generous pinch of saffron
Pinch of salt

Frying and soaking
Frying oil
1 2/3 pounds (800 grams) honey
2 tablespoons orange blossom water
9 ounces (250 grams) toasted sesame seeds, to sprinkle

Preparation

Mix sugar, water, and yeast in a suitable bowl and leave it for 5 minutes. Stir the remaining ingredients in a bowl, then add the yeast mixture until it makes a soft dough. Knead the dough for 8 minutes approximately until smooth, then divide it into 5 parts. Place them in a tray and cover with a plastic wrap. Leave them for 15 minutes. Transfer one portion to a floured surface and spread it into ¼ inch thick. Cut a 3x2 inches rectangles and drizzle flour on top. Roll each rectangle to make a rose shape. Fill a deep pan with oil up to 2 inches and heat up to 350 degrees F. Deep fry the *Chebakia* until golden. Mix honey with blossom water in a pan and heat over medium heat until foamy. Dip the *Chebakia* for 5 minutes in the honey mixture. Then transfer to a plate and garnish with sesame seeds. Serve.

Maakouda

Preparation time: 10 minutes
Cook time: 12 minutes
Nutrition facts (per serving): 297 cal (5g fat, 3g protein, 2g fiber)

Coated and crispy potato cakes, *Maakouda* is known as the classic Moroccan breakfast. It's super and simple to make.

Ingredients (6 servings)
17 1/2 ounces (500 grams) potatoes, boiled and peeled
2 tablespoons chopped parsley
1 ½ teaspoon chopped garlic
½ teaspoon salt or more to taste
¼ teaspoon ground black pepper
Batter
1 teaspoon dried yeast
1 ½ cup (200 grams) flour
½ teaspoon turmeric
½ teaspoon dried garlic grains
½ teaspoon salt
1 cup (200 ml) water
Deep frying oil

Preparation
Mash the potatoes in a bowl and add parsley, garlic, salt, and black pepper then mix well. Make 2 inch in diameter potato cakes from the potato mixture and place them in a tray. Refrigerate the potato cakes until ready to deep fry. Mix yeast with some water in a bowl and leave it for 5 minutes. Stir in the flour, turmeric; garlic powder then mixes well. Leave this batter for 30 minutes. Fill a cooking pot with oil and heat it for deep frying up to 350 degrees F. Coat each potato cake with the flour batter and deep fry for 3 minutes per side. Transfer

to a suitable plate with a paper towel with a slotted spoon. Serve with tomato sauce.

Coconut Ghriba

Preparation time: 15 minutes
Cook time: 20 minutes
Nutrition facts (per serving): 260 cal (17g fat, 10g protein, 13g fiber)

Coconut *Ghriba* is one of the Moroccan specialties, and everyone must try this interesting combination of different sugar and cinnamon toppings.

Ingredients (12 servings)
9 ounces (250 grams) desiccated coconut
2 tablespoons (30 grams) icing sugar
3 1/2 ounces (100 grams) ground almonds
1 teaspoon baking powder
1 teaspoon salt
Zest of one lemon
3 eggs
¼ cup of olive oil
2 tablespoons orange blossom water
1 teaspoon vanilla extract
Melted chocolate, lime zest, dried berries, for decoration

Preparation
At 350 degrees F, preheat your oven. Mix all the dry ingredients for *Ghriba* in a bowl and beat the egg yolks with olive oil, orange blossom water, and vanilla in a bowl until smooth. Beat the egg whites separately in a bowl until fluffy. Add the dry mixture to the egg yolk mixture, mix well, and then fold in egg whites. Layer a baking sheet with parchment paper. Divide the mixture into macaroons balls and place them in the baking tray. Bake the macaroons for 20 minutes until golden. Serve with citrus zest, dried fruits, and melted chocolate on top. Enjoy.

Breakfast Harira

Preparation time: 15 minutes
Cook time: 5 minutes
Nutrition facts (per serving): 162 cal (0g fat, 3g protein, 0.7g fiber)

This breakfast *Harira* is the best way to enjoy semolina porridge in a savory style. Made out of fine semolina and milk, it's a warming delight for your breakfast.

Ingredients (4 servings)
1 cup of fine semolina
2 cups of water
2 tablespoon good quality olive oil
1 teaspoon cumin
1/2 teaspoon salt
1/4 teaspoon black pepper
1 cup of milk

Preparation
Add oil and semolina in a saucepan over medium-high heat. Stir and cook until it gives off its aroma. Stir in cumin, black pepper, and salt. Mix and add water and milk to the semolina. Cook until slightly thick. Serve.

Shakshuka

Preparation time: 10 minutes
Cook time: 37 minutes
Nutrition facts (per serving): 268 cal (2g fat, 19g protein, 0.3g fiber)

Shakshuka is made out of the egg, tomatoes, and spices, and served most commonly in the Moroccan culinary tradition. It's super-rich, healthy, and delicious.

Ingredients (4 servings)
16 ounces (450 grams) kefta
2 tablespoons olive oil
2 garlic cloves, peeled and chopped
1 (400 grams / 14 ounces) can peeled tomatoes, chopped
1 tablespoon chopped fresh parsley
1 teaspoon ground cumin
1 teaspoon paprika
½ teaspoon salt or more to taste
¼ teaspoon ground black pepper
pinch of cayenne pepper
4 eggs
1 teaspoon chopped fresh coriander for garnish

Preparation
Divide the kefta into small meatballs and cover to refrigerate until used. Stir in all the remaining ingredients, except eggs, in a deep skillet. Place it over low heat, cover, and cook for 25 minutes. Add the prepared meatballs to the cooked sauce and cook for 7 minutes. Crack the eggs in the mixture and cook for 5 minutes until the eggs are set. Garnish with coriander. Serve.

Zaalouk Focaccia

Preparation time: 15 minutes
Cook time: 18 minutes
Nutrition facts (per serving): 180 cal (0.1g fat, 8g protein, 1.1g fiber)

If you haven't tried the *Zaalouk Focaccia* before, then here comes a simple and easy to cook recipe that you can prepare at home in no time with minimum efforts.

Ingredients (6 servings)

2 teaspoons dry yeast
1 ½ teaspoon caster sugar
10 1/2 ounces (300 grams) plain flour
7 tablespoons olive oil
1 teaspoon salt
3/4 cup (200 ml) warm water
1 cup *Zaalouk*
A handful of chopped coriander and crumbled feta to serve

Preparation

Mix yeast with sugar and water in a bowl and leave for 5 minutes. Add salt, flour, then mix well. Knead this dough for 10 minutes and then grease a square baking pan with oil. Spread the dough in this baking pan and drizzle 1 ½ tablespoon olive oil on top and spread well. Cover and leave the dough for almost 1 hour. Stretch the dough again and add *Zaalouk* on top. Drizzle remaining oil on top and cover with cling film. Leave for 30 minutes at a warm place. At 420 degrees F, preheat your oven. Bake the focaccia bread for 18 minutes until golden. Garnish with coriander and feta. Serve.

Appetizers
and Snacks

Almond Mhencha

Preparation time: 5 minutes
Cook time: 18 minutes
Nutrition facts (per serving): 231 cal (10g fat, 2g protein, 6g fiber)

Almond *Mhencha* is one of the most delicious appetizers to try. You can opt for different variations for toppings as well.

Ingredients (8 servings)
9 ounces (250 grams) blanched almonds
11/2 tablespoon (20 grams) caster sugar
3 tablespoons orange blossom water
1 tablespoon unsalted butter, softened
Pinch cinnamon
Pinch salt

Pastry
8 sheets filo pastry, 8x12 inch (20 x 30 cm)
3 tablespoons unsalted butter, melted
10 1/2 ounces (300 grams) honey
Groundnuts and freeze-dried berries for decoration

Preparation
At 350 degrees F, preheat your oven. Add sugar and almonds to a food processor and blend well for 5 minutes. Add butter and orange blossom, then blend for 30 seconds. Divide the paste into 8 parts and shape them into tubes. Cover them with a cling film. Spread a filo sheet on a working surface and brush the top with melted butter. Place the almond paste tube on the filo and roll it up. Place this roll in a baking sheet lined with parchment paper. Repeat the same steps with remaining filo sheets and almond paste. Bake the filo rolls for 15 minutes in the oven. Add honey to saucepan and heat over medium heat. Dip the baked rolls

in the honey for 3 minutes then transfer to a serving pan. Garnish with nuts. Serve.

Krachel

Preparation time: 15 minutes
Cook time: 25 minutes
Nutrition facts (per serving): 230 cal (4.2g fat, 10g protein, 1.4g fiber)

If you haven't tried the *Krachel* before, then here comes a simple and easy recipe that you can easily prepare and cook at home successfully.

Ingredients (8 servings)
2 tablespoons toasted sesame
1 teaspoon aniseed
2 teaspoons dry active yeast
4 tablespoons (60 grams) caster sugar
10 1/2 ounces (300 grams) flour
1/2 teaspoon salt
1 egg
1/2 cup (120 ml) warm milk
1 2/3 ounces (50 grams) unsalted butter, melted
1 tablespoon orange blossom water
1 egg yolk for brushing

Preparation
Mix yeast with sugar, warm water in a bowl and leave it for 10 minutes. Mix flour, sesame seeds, aniseed, and salt in a bowl and stir in milk, the yeast mixture, and orange blossom water then mix well until it makes a sticky dough. Knead this dough for 15 minutes, then transfer to a greased bowl and cover it with a cling film then leave it for 1 hour. Divide this dough into 8 small balls and place them in a baking sheet. Cover again and leave for 20 minutes. At 350 degrees F, preheat your oven. Brush the balls with egg yolk and drizzle sesame seeds on top. Bake for 25 minutes until golden brown. Serve warm.

Fekkas

Preparation time: 10 minutes
Cook time: 15 minutes
Nutrition facts (per serving): 130 cal (8g fat, 2g protein, 1.1g fiber)

If you can't think of anything to cook and make in a short time, then try this Moroccan biscuit appetizer because it has great taste and texture to serve.

Ingredients (15 servings)
3 eggs
7 1/2 ounces (200 grams) caster sugar
9 ounces (250 grams) plain flour
¼ teaspoon salt
½ tablespoon baking powder
3 1/2 ounces (100 grams) dried cranberries
3 1/2 ounces (100 grams) unsalted shelled pistachios
3 1/2 ounces (100 grams) roasted almonds
Zest of a lemon
3 1/2 ounces (100 grams) white chocolate, melted (for decoration, optional)
Sprinkles (for decoration, optional)

Preparation
At 350 degrees F, preheat your oven. Beat eggs with sugar in a bowl with an electric beater until foamy. Mix the remaining ingredients in a bowl except for sprinkles and white chocolate. Stir in egg mixture and mix well to get a dough. Divide this dough into 3 equal pieces. Roll each piece into a 2 inch thick cylinder. Place the rolls in a baking sheet lined with parchment paper. Bake them for 35 minutes until golden brown. Remove it from the oven and allow it to cool. Reduce the oven's heat to 300 degrees F. Slice the cylinders into thick biscottis and return them to the baking sheet. Bake the biscottis for 15 until golden brown in the oven. Serve.

Amlou

Preparation time: 15 minutes
Nutrition facts (per serving): 106 cal (9g fat, 4g protein, 0.1g fiber)

The appetizing *Amlou* makes a great addition to the menu, and they look great when served at the table.

Ingredients (12 servings)
9 ounces (250 grams) roasted unpeeled almonds
1/4 cup (80 ml) argan oil
1/4 cup (80 ml) honey
½ teaspoon flaky salt, such as Maldon
Generous sprinkle of cinnamon

Preparation
Blend the almonds with oil, honey, and salt in a blender until smooth. Garnish with cinnamon. Serve.

Orange Scones

Preparation time: 15 minutes
Cook time: 18 minutes
Nutrition facts (per serving): 101 cal (11g fat, 7g protein, 3g fiber)

If you haven't tried these orange scones, then you since they have no parallel in taste and texture.

Ingredients (6 servings)
8 ounces (225 grams) self-rising flour
½ teaspoon salt
Zest of 1 orange
1 teaspoon ground cardamom
4 tablespoons (60 grams) unsalted cold butter, cut into 1/3 inch cubes
3 tablespoons (40 grams) caster sugar
1/2 cup (150 ml) milk
Beaten egg for egg wash

Preparation
At 390 degrees F, preheat your oven. Dust a baking sheet with flour. Mix butter, orange zest, cardamom, salt, and flour in a large bowl. Stir in the sugar and remaining ingredients before you mix well. Knead for 1 minute and then roll into 2/3 inch thick sheet. Cut scones out of this dough using a pastry cutter. Place the scones in a baking sheet and brush with beaten egg. Bake the scones for 18 minutes until golden brown. Serve.

Olive Tapenade

Preparation time: 10 minutes
Nutrition facts (per serving): 202 cal (4g fat, 11g protein, 9g fiber)

Who doesn't like to have an olive tapenade? Olive lovers love them on the menu, so this tapenade is a must!

Ingredients (6 servings)
1 cup (200 grams) black cured olives
2 tablespoons capers, rinsed and drained
2 garlic cloves, chopped
1 tablespoon harissa
1 tablespoon lemon juice
1 tablespoon parsley
1/4 cup olive oil

Preparation
Mix the olives with capers and process in the food processer until it makes a chunky paste. Add the remaining ingredients and mix well. Serve.

Ham Cheese Empanadas

Preparation time: 15 minutes
Cook time: 24 minutes
Nutrition facts (per serving): 232 cal (11g fat, 13g protein, 3g fiber)

These cheese empanadas will satisfy your ham and cheese cringe in no time. They're quick to make and bake if you have ready to serve dough at home.

Ingredients (6 servings)
2 tablespoons butter
1/2 cup flour
1 cup milk
2 eggs
1/2 cup smoked Gouda cheese, grated
4 tablespoons Parmesan, grated
1 pinch cayenne pepper
1 pinch salt
1 package puff pastry dough
1/4-pound ham
1 egg yolk
1 tablespoon water

Preparation
At 400 degrees F, preheat your oven. Add butter to a suitable saucepan and melt over medium-low heat. Stir in flour and mix to cook for 2 minutes. Add milk and mix until it makes a thick sauce. Add 2 eggs and cook for 2 minutes with occasional stirring. Stir in the Parmesan, Gouda, salt, and cayenne pepper. Spread 1 sheet of puff pastry into a 12 inch, square on a floured surface. Cut the sheet into 12 3x4 inches rectangles. Beat egg yolk with water in a bowl. Brush the rectangles with egg yolk mixture. Top half with ham and 2 tablespoon cheese sauce. Place the remaining rectangles on top. Press the edges of the dough rectangles to seal and place on a baking sheet lined with parchment paper. Brush

their top with the egg yolk mixture. Bake for almost 20 minutes until golden brown. Serve warm.

Moroccan Chickpeas Quinoa

Preparation time: 15 minutes
Nutrition facts (per serving): 196 cal (3g fat, 12g protein, 3g fiber)

Moroccan chickpea quinoa is another Moroccan-inspired delight that you should definitely try. Serve with the flavorsome sauce.

Ingredients (8 servings)
2 cups cooked quinoa
2/3 cup canned chickpeas
1/3 cup chopped onion
4 cups leafy greens
2/3 cup diced tomatoes
1/2 cup crumbled feta cheese
4 figs, dried
1 cup carrot, diced
1-ounce pistachios

Dressing
1/4 cup olive oil
2 tablespoon balsamic vinegar
1 splash of lemon juice
2 teaspoon honey
¼ teaspoon ground paprika
1/4 teaspoon cumin
Salt and pepper to taste
1/4 cup chopped parsley leaves
2 tablespoon chopped mint

Preparation
Add chickpeas, turmeric, ginger, and pepper to a bowl. Stir in the quinoa and mix well. Toss in the remaining ingredients and serve.

Bessara

Preparation time: 10 minutes
Cook time: 1 hour
Nutrition facts (per serving): 101 cal (3g fat, 14g protein, 4g fiber)

Bessara is a fava bean dip that can be served with an appetizer, snack, or entrées. It's full of nutrients and your favorite spices.

Ingredients (2 servings)
1 1/2 cups dried fava beans
2 cloves garlic, or to taste
1/3 cup olive oil
1/4 cup lemon juice
2 tablespoons reserved cooking liquid
1 1/2 teaspoons salt
1 teaspoon ground cumin
1/2 teaspoon sweet paprika
1/2 teaspoon hot paprika
Chopped parsley to garnish

Preparation
Soak the fava beans in cold overnight, drain, and rinse. Transfer the beans to a pot with water to boil for 1 hour or more until beans are soft. Drain and reserve its cooking liquid. Blend the beans with remaining ingredients and 2 tablespoons of the cooking liquid until smooth. Garnish with parsley. Serve.

Salads

Tangy Couscous Salad

Preparation time: 10 minutes
Cook time: 10 minutes
Nutrition facts (per serving): 164 cal (12g fat, 8g protein, 2.1g fiber)

Tangy couscous salad is the best salad to find in Moroccan cuisine. It's packed with nutrients as it's prepared with couscous, feta cheese, and courgettes.

Ingredients (8 servings)
10 ½ ounces (300 grams) couscous, cooked
2 courgettes, thinly sliced
1 tablespoon olive oil
3 1/2 ounces (100 grams) feta cheese, crumbled
½ ounce parsley, chopped
Juice 1 lemon

Preparation
Sauté the courgettes with olive oil in a griddle pan until a little crispy. Stir in the couscous, feta cheese, parsley, and lemon juice. Mix and cook for almost 2 minutes and then serve. Enjoy.

Tabbouleh salad

Preparation time: 15 minutes
Nutrition facts (per serving): 244 cal (6g fat, 8g protein, 5g fiber)

If you haven't tried the tabbouleh salad, then here comes a simple and easy to cook recipe to recreate at home in no time with minimum efforts.

Ingredients (6 servings)

9 ounces (250 grams) couscous, cooked
4 vine-ripened tomatoes, chopped
½ cucumber, peeled and chopped
1 bunch spring onions, sliced
1-ounce fresh parsley, chopped
Grated zest of 1 lemon
6 tablespoons olive oil
2 tablespoons lemon juice
1 crushed garlic clove

Preparation

Toss the couscous with all other salad ingredients in a salad bowl. Serve.

Moroccan Carrot, Chickpea, and Almond Salad

Preparation time: 15 minutes
Cook time: 2 minutes
Nutrition facts (per serving): 146 cal (11g fat, 9g protein, 4.1g fiber)

This almond and chickpea salad is everyone's favorite go-to meal when it comes to serving; you can prepare them in no time without any cooking.

Ingredients (8 servings)
For the dressing
1 teaspoon cumin seeds
1 teaspoon coriander seeds
1/3 cup olive oil
3 tablespoons fresh lemon juice
½ teaspoon salt, or to taste

For the salad
2 large carrots, julienned
2 cups chickpeas, cooked and drained
6 dried apricot halves, sliced
4 black dried figs, sliced
1/3 cup sliced, toasted almonds
Fresh mint and dill, torn

Preparation
Sauté coriander seeds and cumin seeds in a skillet for 2 minutes and then transfer to a mortar. Grind with a pestle and add olive oil, lemon juice, and salt then mix well. Toss all the almond salad ingredients in a salad bowl and then add the prepared the dressing. Mix and serve.

Charred Green Pepper Lemon Salad

Preparation time: 10 minutes
Nutrition facts (per serving): 60 cal (7g fat, 0g protein, 2g fiber)

The green pepper lemon salad makes a great side. Plus, you can serve them a delicious snack as well. These are loved for their crispy coating and creamy taste.

Ingredients (2 servings)
1 green pepper roasted and skin removed
1/4 preserved lemon
Moroccan salad vinaigrette

Preparation
Toss all the lemon salad ingredients in a salad bowl then serve.

Moroccan Carrot Salad

Preparation time: 10 minutes
Cook time: 15 minutes
Nutrition facts (per serving): 201 cal (16g fat, 6g protein, 6g fiber)

The Moroccan carrot salad is another most popular salad in Moroccan Cuisine, and it has a great taste from the mix of carrots and spices.

Ingredients (4 servings)

1/2 lb. carrots, peeled
1/4 cup vinegar
1/2 cup olive oil
1/2 teaspoon salt
1/2 teaspoon black pepper
1/2 teaspoon crushed garlic

Preparation

Add the peeled carrots to boiling water, cook for 15 minutes, and then transfer to a bowl. Cut the carrots into ovals and transfer to a salad bowl. Add vinegar, oil, salt, black pepper, and garlic to the bowl. Mix and serve.

Orange Olive Salad with Argan Dressing

Preparation time: 10 minutes
Nutrition facts (per serving): 211 cal (10g fat, 4g protein, 13g fiber)

An orange olive salad is the right fit to serve with all your Moroccan entrees. Here the oranges and orange juice are mixed with veggies and a paprika dressing for a wholesome flavor.

Ingredients (2 servings)
2 1/2 medium oranges, peeled and cut into segments
6 black salted olives
1 teaspoon chopped cilantro
1/8 teaspoon paprika
1/8 teaspoon cumin
1/2 teaspoon crushed garlic
2 teaspoon argan oil
1/8 cup orange juice

Preparation
Toss all the olive salad ingredients in a salad bowl and then serve.

Zaalouk Eggplant Salad

Preparation time: 10 minutes
Cook time: 15 minutes
Nutrition facts (per serving): 253 cal (2g fat, 11g protein, 4g fiber)

Zaalouk is an eggplant salad, which has a refreshing taste due to the use of mint in it. It's great to serve with skewers and as a bread topping.

Ingredients (4 servings)
1 large cubed eggplant
1 tomato, chopped
1 small chopped onion
1/4 cup olive oil
2 cloves garlic chopped
2 teaspoons paprika
2 teaspoons cumin
Salt and pepper to taste
1/2 lemon
Chopped cilantro

Preparation
Place a suitable frying pan with oil on medium heat. Stir in the onion and garlic and then sauté for 5 minutes. Add half of the spices, eggplant, and tomatoes. Stir in tomato sauce and sauté until soft. Garnish with cilantro and lemon juice. Enjoy.

Taktouka

Preparation time: 10 minutes
Cook time: 10 minutes
Nutrition facts (per serving): 179 cal (16g fat, 5g protein, 3g fiber)

Taktouka is quite a special green peppers salad, and a must to serve with all the different entrees. Use this quick and simple recipe to prepare in no time.

Ingredients (4 servings)
4 tomatoes, peeled and chopped
2 large green peppers, roasted
1 large garlic clove, chopped
1 teaspoon salt
1/2 teaspoon black pepper
1 tablespoon paprika
2 teaspoons cumin
1/4 teaspoon turmeric
1/3 cup olive oil

Preparation
Toss all the *Taktouka* salad ingredients in a suitable pan, sauté for 10 minutes, transfer to a salad bowl, and then serve.

Potato, Carrot and Rice Salad

Preparation time: 10 minutes
Nutrition facts (per serving): 176 cal (17g fat, 7g protein, 3g fiber)

The Moroccan menu is incomplete without a potato carrot salad. It's made from potatoes, carrots, and rice, which add lots of nutritional value.

Ingredients (4 servings)
3 medium potatoes, boiled and cubed
2 carrots, peeled and chopped
3/4 cup of rice, cooked
1 tablespoon mayo
1/2 teaspoon cumin
Salt and pepper to taste

Preparation
Toss all the rice salad ingredients in a salad bowl and then serve.

Tomato and Onion Salad

Preparation time: 10 minutes
Nutrition facts (per serving): 155 cal (8g fat, 3g protein, 2g fiber)

Ingredients (4 servings)
2 large, fresh tomatoes, peeled and chopped
1/2 sweet onion, sliced
1 1/2 tablespoon white vinegar
3 tablespoon cup olive oil
1/2 teaspoon salt
1/2 teaspoon black pepper

Preparation
Toss all the tomato and onion salad ingredients in a salad bowl and then serve.

Sweet Tomato Salad

Preparation time: 10 minutes
Cook time: 15 minutes
Nutrition facts (per serving): 150 cal (4g fat, 1g protein, 2g fiber)

This salad is something that you can serve with every other meal. It goes well with bread for brunches, soups, rices, and curries as well.

Ingredients (4 servings)
4 medium tomatoes, peeled and chopped
1 teaspoon vegetable oil
1 tablespoon butter
1/2 teaspoon cinnamon
1/2 teaspoon salt

Preparation
Toss all the sweet tomato salad ingredients in a suitable pan and cook on low heat for 15 minutes until the tomatoes are soft. Serve.

Loubia Salad in Tomato Sauce

Preparation time: 10 minutes
Cook time: 5 minutes
Nutrition facts (per serving): 243 cal (13g fat, 5g protein, 2g fiber)

Loubia salad has an interesting name and an amazing taste as well. It has a mix of cannellini beans, tomato sauce, and spices.

Ingredients (4 servings)
1 cup cannellini beans, boiled
2 teaspoon olive oil
3/4 cup tomato sauce
1/2 onion chopped
1 handful Italian parsley, chopped
2 garlic cloves, crushed
1/2 teaspoon turmeric
1/2 teaspoon salt
1 teaspoon cumin
1/4 teaspoon red pepper

Preparation
Toss all the Loubia salad ingredients in a cooking pot and cook for 5 minutes on medium heat. Serve.

Moroccan Zucchini Salad

Preparation time: 15 minutes
Cook time: 10 minutes
Nutrition facts (per serving): 181 cal (5g fat, 7g protein, 6g fiber)

If you haven't tried the Moroccan Zucchini Salad before, then here comes a simple and easy to cook a recipe that you can recreate at home in no time with minimum efforts.

Ingredients (4 servings)
1-pound (1/2 kilogram) zucchini
1/2 teaspoon salt
1 large egg
2 teaspoon olive oil
1/2 teaspoon crushed garlic
1 tablespoon cumin
Pinch of paprika

Preparation
Place the zucchini in a colander and drizzle salt on top then leave it for 30 minutes. Sauté garlic with oil in a skillet for 45 seconds. Stir in the zucchini and sauté until combined. Beat egg in a small bowl. Pour into the zucchini and mix well. Add spices and cook with occasional stirring for 4 minutes. Garnish with parsley. Serve warm.

Soups

Moroccan Harira

Preparation time: 15 minutes
Cook time: 60 minutes
Nutrition facts (per serving): 451 cal (14g fat, 26g protein, 18g fiber)

The Moroccan *Harira* is a delight to serve during winters. It's known for its healing effects and offers a very energizing combination of ingredients.

Ingredients (12 servings)
3 tablespoons vegetable oil
1/2-pound lamb
6 large tomatoes, peeled, seeded, and pureed
1 tablespoon salt
1/2 teaspoon turmeric
1 bunch parsley, chopped
1 bunch cilantro, chopped
1 stalk celery, chopped
1 1/2 teaspoons pepper
1 teaspoon ground cinnamon
1 tablespoon ground ginger
1 large onion, grated
1 handful dried chickpeas, soaked overnight
1 tablespoon smen
11 cups water
3 tablespoons dried lentils, soaked overnight
3 tablespoons tomato paste
2 tablespoons rice

For Thickening
1 cup flour
2 cups of water
1 tablespoon chopped parsley

Preparation

Add oil and meat to a pressure cooker and sauté until brown. Stir in salt, tomatoes, parsley, turmeric, cilantro, celery, pepper, cinnamon, onion, smen, chickpeas, and ginger, along with 3 cups of water. Put on the lid and cook for 30 minutes on high pressure. Add the lentils, tomato paste, rice, and 8 cups water; then put on the lid and pressure cook for 30 minutes. Release the pressure slowly. Mix flour with water in a suitable bowl and pour into the soup then continue to cook on low heat until it thickens. Garnish with parsley. Serve warm.

Moroccan Vegetable Soup

Preparation time: 10 minutes
Cook time: 60 minutes
Nutrition facts (per serving): 330 cal (8g fat, 18g protein, 21g fiber)

Try this Moroccan vegetable soup with your favorite herbs on top. Adding a dollop of cream or yogurt will make it even richer in taste.

Ingredients (8 servings)

4 tablespoons olive oil
1 large onion, diced
1/2 teaspoon ground turmeric
3 stalks celery, diced
3 large carrots, peeled and sliced
1 teaspoon ground cumin
1 teaspoon harissa
Salt to taste
1 bunch parsley, chopped
1 bunch cilantro, chopped
1 (15-ounce/425 grams) can tomatoes, crushed
1 cup (200 grams) chickpeas, cooked
1 cup (370 grams) green lentils
7 cups (1 2/3 liters) chicken stock
1 teaspoon freshly ground black pepper
2 tablespoons all-purpose flour
1 large egg
Juice of 2 lemons

Preparation

Sauté the onion, carrots, and celery with oil in a skillet for 10 minutes until soft. Stir in the harissa, salt, parsley, cilantro, cumin, turmeric, tomatoes, and stock, then cook to a boil. Add chickpeas and cook for 25 minutes on a simmer. Stir in the lentils and cook for another 20 minutes. Mix flour with 2 cups water, lemon juice, and egg in a bowl then pour into the soup. Cook on a simmer for 5 minutes with occasional stirring. Garnish with parsley and cilantro. Serve warm.

Moroccan Potato Bean Soup

Preparation time: 10 minutes
Cook time: 20 minutes
Nutrition facts (per serving): 367 cal (6g fat, 9g protein, 1.2g fiber)

Try this super tasty Moroccan potato beans soup for your meals, and you'll never stop having it. That's how heavenly the combination tastes.

Ingredients (8 servings)
6 cups of water
1 (15 ounces) can kidney beans
3 tablespoons olive oil
2 medium onions, chopped
2 medium potatoes, peeled and cubed
3 tablespoons chicken bouillon powder
½ teaspoon ground turmeric
½ teaspoon ground black pepper
½ teaspoon ground white pepper
½ teaspoon cayenne pepper
2 teaspoons curry powder
2 tablespoons soy sauce
½ cup whole milk
½ cup half-and-half
½ cup dry potato flakes
¼ cup chopped green onions

Preparation
Boil the white kidney beans with water for 15 minutes and then drain. Sauté the onion with olive oil in a cooking pot until golden brown. Stir in the potatoes, chicken soup-based potatoes, soy sauce, turmeric, all the spices, and then cook until the potatoes are soft. Stir in the remaining ingredients, cook to a boil, and then serve warm.

Moroccan Chickpea Soup

Preparation time: 10 minutes
Cook time: 20 minutes
Nutrition facts (per serving): 384 cal (5g fat, 14g protein, 12g fiber)

Enjoy this Moroccan chickpea soup with mixed lemon flavors. Adding broad beans to the soup delivers a very strong taste with all the herbs and spices.

Ingredients (6 servings)
1 tablespoon olive oil
1 onion, chopped
2 celery sticks, chopped
2 teaspoon ground cumin
2 1/4 cups (600 ml) hot vegetable stock
14 ounces (400 grams) can plum tomatoes, chopped
14 ounces (400 grams) can chickpeas, rinsed and drained
3 1/2 ounces (100 grams) frozen broad beans
Zest and juice ½ lemon
Large handful coriander or parsley and flatbread, to serve

Preparation
Sauté the onion and celery with oil in a cooking pot for 10 minutes until softened. Stir in the cumin and fry for 1 minute more. Turn up the heat and add tomatoes, stock, chickpeas, and black pepper. Let it simmer for 8 minutes. Add in the broad beans and lemon juice, cook for another 2 minutes. Garnish with lemon zest and chopped herbs. Serve warm with flatbread.

Moroccan Chicken Soup

Preparation time: 10 minutes
Cook time: 45 minutes
Nutrition facts (per serving): 479 cal (11g fat, 32g protein, 6g fiber)

Make this Moroccan chicken soup in no time and enjoy it with some garnish on top. Adding crispy bread on top makes it super tasty.

Ingredients (8 servings)
2 tablespoon olive oil
1 1/2 teaspoon salt, divided
1/4 teaspoon black pepper
2 boneless, skinless chicken breasts
2 carrots, peeled and diced
2 ribs celery, diced
1 small onion, chopped
3 garlic cloves, minced
1 teaspoon minced ginger
1 1/2 teaspoon ground cumin
1 1/2 teaspoon ground coriander
1 teaspoon turmeric
1/2 teaspoon cinnamon
1/4 teaspoon cayenne pepper
1 tablespoon tomato paste
7 cups of water
1 (19 ounces) can of chickpeas, drained and rinsed
2 1/2 tablespoon lemon juice
1 tablespoon chopped cilantro, for serving

Preparation
Rub all the chicken breasts with salt and black pepper and sear it for 4 minutes per side with olive oil in a pan. Stir in the carrots, celery and onion, then sauté

for 5 minutes. Add ginger, garlic, spices, and salt. Sauté for 1 minute. Add tomato paste to hot pan and cook for 1 minute. Pour in water and cook to a boil. Reduce the pan's heat and cook for 40 minutes on a simmer. Shred the chicken with two forks and add the chickpeas and lemon juice. Garnish with cilantro and serve warm.

Saffron Chorba

Preparation time: 15 minutes
Cook time: 80 minutes
Nutrition facts (per serving): 336 cal (2g fat, 33 protein, 12g fiber)

Saffron *Chorba* is quite famous in the region; in fact, and it's a must to try because of its nutritional content.

Ingredients (6 servings)
2 large sweet potatoes, peeled, and diced
2 large eggplant/aubergine, diced
2 tablespoons olive oil
2 onions, sliced
2 tomatoes, grated
2 tablespoons tomato paste
½ teaspoon ground turmeric
2 very generous pinches of saffron
1 teaspoon salt or more to taste
½ teaspoon ground black pepper
2 cups (500 ml) vegetable stock
1 (14 ounces) can chickpeas, rinsed
3 1/2 ounces (100 grams) spaghetti broken into 3 cm long pieces
Chopped parsley and more for serving

Preparation
At 392 degrees F, preheat your oven. Spread the aubergine or eggplant and the sweet potato in a large roasting tray and then drizzle some olive oil and salt on top. Bake it in the preheated oven and roast for about 25 to 30 minutes until tender. Set aside until ready to use. Sauté the onions, tomatoes, turmeric, saffron, tomato paste, salt, and black pepper with olive oil in a casserole pan for 10 minutes on medium heat. Stir in the water and stock and cook to a boil. Reduce its heat to medium-low and cover to cook for 40 minutes. Add

chickpeas and boil again. Stir in the sweet potato, eggplant/aubergine, and spaghetti; then cook until the spaghetti is soft. Garnish with parsley. Serve warm.

Loubia Stew

Preparation time: 10 minutes
Cook time: 35 minutes
Nutrition facts (per serving): 367 cal (8g fat, 27g protein, 3g fiber)

This stew is everything I was looking for. The beans, tomatoes, and kale make a complete package for any health enthusiast.

Ingredients (6 servings)
2 cans cannellini beans, rinsed and drained
2 tomatoes grated
1 large onion, sliced
3/4 cup (200 ml) vegetable stock
3 1/2 ounces (100 grams) sundried tomato, chopped
11/2 tablespoon (20 grams) kale, chopped
3 tablespoons olive oil
2 garlic cloves, peeled and crushed
2 teaspoons turmeric
2 teaspoons paprika
½ teaspoon salt or more to taste
½ teaspoon ground black pepper
3 tablespoons chopped fresh parsley for garnish

Preparation
Whisk and mix all the ingredients in a large suitable saucepan over medium heat. Cook to a boil and then reduce the heat to low. Cover and cook on a simmer for 35 minutes with occasional stirring. Serve warm.

Chicken Chorba

Preparation time: 15 minutes
Cook time: 65 minutes
Nutrition facts (per serving): 386 cal (3g fat, 24g protein, 5g fiber)

You won't know until you try it! That's what people told me about Chicken Chorba, and it indeed tasted more unique and flavorful than other soups I've tried.

Ingredients (6 servings)
1 tablespoon olive oil
2 onions, sliced
2 pounds (1 kg) of chicken wings
2 teaspoons turmeric
Generous pinch saffron threads
1 teaspoon salt or more to taste
½ teaspoon ground black pepper
5 ounces (150 grams) dried chickpeas, overnight and drained
2 medium-sized tomatoes, grated
1 ½ tablespoon tomato paste
2 large white potatoes (500 grams), diced
3 1/2 ounces (100 grams) spaghetti, broken
3 tablespoons parsley, chopped

Preparation
Sauté the onion, chicken, spices, salt, and black pepper in a casserole dish for 10 minutes, then add water and chickpeas. Cook the mixture to a boil, then reduce the heat to medium-low and cook for 40 minutes on a simmer. Add the potatoes, tomato paste, and tomatoes, then cook to a boil. Cover and cook again for 15 minutes. Add the parsley and spaghetti pieces then cook until the spaghetti is soft. Garnish with parsley.

Berkoukech

Preparation time: 15 minutes
Cook time: 90 minutes
Nutrition facts (per serving): 482 cal (4g fat, 28g protein, 3g fiber)

Ingredients (6 servings)
1 tablespoon olive oil
1 onion, grated
7 1/2 ounces (200 grams) braising beef, cubed
2 medium-sized tomatoes, grated
2 tablespoons chopped coriander
1 teaspoon tomato paste
½ teaspoon ground ginger
A pinch of saffron
1 ½ teaspoon salt or more to taste
¼ ground black pepper
7 1/2 ounces (200 grams) carrots, chopped
3 1/2 ounces (100 grams) celery, chopped
3 1/2 ounces (100 grams) drained canned chickpeas
7 1/2 ounces (200 grams) courgette, chopped
5 ounces (150grams) giant couscous

Preparation
Sauté the onions, meat, tomatoes, spices, salt, black pepper, tomato paste, coriander with oil in a casserole pan for 10 minutes until meat is brown. Stir in carrots, celery, and water, then cook to a boil. Reduce its heat to low, cover, and cook for 60 minutes on a simmer. Add the chickpeas and courgette and cook for another 20 minutes. Add the couscous and cook for 9 minutes. Garnish with coriander. Serve.

Moroccan Cauliflower Soup

Preparation time: 15 minutes
Cook time: 22 minutes
Nutrition facts (per serving): 358 cal (14g fat, 9g protein, 4g fiber)

Vegan can give the soup a try because it has a good and delicious combination of cauliflower, almond, and harissa.

Ingredients (6 servings)
1 large cauliflower
2 tablespoon olive oil
½ teaspoon ground cinnamon
½ teaspoon cumin
½ teaspoon coriander
2 tablespoon harissa paste
4 cups hot vegetable stock
2 tablespoons toasted flaked almond

Preparation
Sauté the cauliflower florets with olive oil, cinnamon, cumin, coriander, and harissa paste for 2 minutes. Stir in the almonds and stock and cover to cook for 20 minutes. Blend this soup until smooth and garnish with almond and harissa. Serve warm.

Fish Stew

Preparation time: 15 minutes
Cook time: 15 minutes
Nutrition facts (per serving): 441 cal (11g fat, 34g protein, 5g fiber)

This fish stew is loved by all, young and adult. It's simple and quick to make. This delight is great to serve at dinner tables.

Ingredients (6 servings)
1 tablespoon olive oil
1 onion, chopped
1 pinch saffron
2 1/4 cups (600 ml) hot fish stock
2 garlic cloves, crushed
1 thumb-sized piece ginger, peeled and grated
½ green chili, finely sliced
2 teaspoon ground cumin
1 teaspoon ground coriander
1 teaspoon cinnamon
1 tablespoon tomato purée
10 cherry tomatoes, halved
2 tablespoon ground almonds
Zest 1 orange, juice of ½
1 tablespoon honey
1 1/2 pounds (700 grams) white fish, diced
1 small bunch coriander, chopped
1 handful flaked almond, toasted
½ green chili, deseeded
Couscous and natural yogurt, to serve

Preparation

Add saffron to the hot stock and let it steep. Sauté the onion with oil in a stockpot until soft. Add garlic, chili, and ginger, then sauté for 1 minute. Stir in spices, tomatoes puree, tomatoes, almonds, orange zest and juice, saffron stock, and honey, then cook for 10 minutes on a simmer. Add the fish to the soup, cover, and cook on low heat for 3 minutes. Add coriander, toasted almond, and coriander. Serve warm.

Main Dishes

Moroccan Spiced Salmon

Preparation time: 5 minutes
Cook time: 12 minutes
Nutrition facts (per serving): 378 cal (14g fat, 31g protein, 0.7g fiber)

Try the spiced salmon for dinner as the fish is infused with an amazing blend of Moroccan spices. Serve warm with your favorite sauces.

Ingredients (4 servings)
¾ teaspoon ground cinnamon
¾ teaspoon ground cumin
½ teaspoon salt
½ teaspoon ground ginger
¼ teaspoon mustard powder
¼ teaspoon ground nutmeg
⅛ teaspoon cayenne pepper
⅛ teaspoon ground allspice
2 teaspoons white sugar
2 pounds (1-inch thick) boneless, skin-on center-cut salmon fillets
1 tablespoon fresh lime juice

Preparation
Mix all the spices, sugar, and lime juice in a suitable bowl. Place the salmon in a baking tray and liberally rub the spice mix on top. Leave it to marinate for 40 minutes. At 425 degrees F, preheat your oven. Roast the salmon for 12 minutes in the oven then leave it for 15 minutes. Serve.

Lamb Lentil Stew

Preparation time: 5 minutes
Cook time: 45 minutes
Nutrition facts (per serving): 436 cal (14.3g fat, 33g protein, 8g fiber)

This lamb stew is a typical Moroccan entree, which is a must to have on the Moroccan menu. It has this rich mix of lentils, sweet potatoes, and beans that I love.

Ingredients (6 servings)
1 teaspoon ground cinnamon
1 teaspoon ground cumin
½ teaspoon ground ginger
¼ teaspoon ground cloves
¼ teaspoon ground nutmeg
¼ teaspoon ground turmeric
⅛ teaspoon curry powder
1 teaspoon salt
1-pound ground lamb
1 tablespoon butter
1 sweet onion, chopped
1 (14.5 ounces) can organic beef broth
1 (14.5 ounces) can organic chicken broth
2 (14.5 ounce) cans beef consommé
1 (14.5 ounces) can diced tomatoes, undrained
1 tablespoon honey
3 large carrots, chopped
2 small sweet potato, peeled and diced
1 (15 ounces) can garbanzo beans, rinsed
½ cup chopped dried apricots
1 cup dried lentils, rinsed
Ground black pepper, to taste

Preparation

Mix ground lamb with all the spices and refrigerate overnight. Add and melt the butter in a large pot over medium heat. Stir in the onion and sauté for 10 minutes. Add spice lamb and cook for 5 minutes. Add chicken and beef broth, consommé, honey, tomatoes, beans, lentils, apricots, sweet potatoes, and carrot. Cook to a boil then reduce the heat to low. Cook the stew for 30 minutes then serve warm.

Shabbat Fish

Preparation time: 5 minutes
Cook time: 60 minutes
Nutrition facts (per serving): 394 cal (14g fat, 36g protein, 0g fiber)

Simple and easy to make, this recipe is a must to try on this menu. Shabbat fish is a delight for the dinner table.

Ingredients (6 servings)
1 red bell pepper, julienned
3 tomatoes, sliced
6 (6 ounces) tilapia fillets
2 tablespoons paprika
1 tablespoon chicken bouillon granules
1 teaspoon cayenne pepper
Salt and pepper to taste
¼ cup olive oil
1 cup of water
¼ cup chopped fresh parsley

Preparation
At 200 degrees F, preheat your oven. Spread the tomatoes and red pepper in a baking dish and place the tilapia fillets on top. Mix the paprika, chicken bouillon, all the spices, olive oil, and water in a bowl and pour over the fish. Add parsley on top and cover the dish with a foil. Bake it for 1 hour in the oven. Serve warm.

Moroccan Black-Eyed Peas

Preparation time: 5 minutes
Cook time: 1 hour 30 minutes
Nutrition facts (per serving): 278 cal (11g fat, 12g protein, 4g fiber)

Moroccan black-eyed peas are one of the traditional entrées.

Ingredients (4 servings)
1½ cups dried black-eyed peas
1 onion, chopped
1 (8 ounces) can tomato sauce
½ cup olive oil
¼ cup chopped fresh cilantro
3 garlic cloves, chopped
1½ teaspoons salt
1½ teaspoon ground cumin
1½ teaspoon sweet paprika
1 teaspoon ground ginger
¼ teaspoon cayenne pepper
3½ cups water

Preparation
Soak the black-eyed peas in cool water for 8 hours or overnight, then rinse. Transfer the peas, onion, and all other ingredients to a stockpot, and cook to a boil. Reduce its heat, cover, and cook for 1 ½ hour on a simmer. Serve warm.

Moroccan Shrimp Tagine

Preparation time: 5 minutes
Cook time: 32 minutes
Nutrition facts (per serving): 292 cal (13g fat, 31g protein, 0.8g fiber)

A perfect mix of shrimp, carrots, and saffron is all that you need to expand your Moroccan menu. Simple and easy to make, this recipe is unforgettable!

Ingredients (6 servings)
3 tablespoons olive oil
4 large carrots, chopped
1 large sweet onion, diced
1 large russet potato, peeled and diced
1 red bell pepper, thinly sliced
½ cup pitted Kalamata olives, sliced
2 tablespoons minced garlic
2 teaspoons ginger paste
2 large tomatoes, coarsely chopped
½ cup chopped fresh cilantro
1 tablespoon dried parsley
2 teaspoons ground cumin
2 teaspoons seasoned salt
1 (1.41 ounce) package sazon seasoning with saffron
1 teaspoon paprika
1 teaspoon ground turmeric
1 teaspoon lemon juice
½ teaspoon cayenne pepper
½ teaspoon ground black pepper
1 bay leaf
1-pound uncooked medium shrimp, peeled and deveined

Preparation

Sauté the carrots, onion, potato, and bell pepper with olive oil in a Dutch oven for 5 minutes, then add olives, ginger, garlic paste and sauté for 2 minutes. Add cumin, parsley, cilantro, tomatoes, salt, paprika, turmeric, lemon juice, cayenne, sazon, black pepper, and bay leaf. Cover and cook for 20 minutes on a simmer. Stir in the shrimp and cook for 5 minutes. Serve warm.

Moroccan Chicken Stew

Preparation time: 15 minutes
Cook time: 53 minutes
Nutrition facts (per serving): 473 cal (11g fat, 36g protein, 2g fiber)

Do you want to enjoy chicken stew with a Moroccan twist? Then try this Moroccan chicken stew recipe. You can serve it with your favorite dips and sauces.

Ingredients (6 servings)
1 large handful flaked almonds, toasted
1 tablespoon ghee
2 red onions, sliced
4 garlic cloves, chopped
1 thumb-sized piece ginger, finely grated
4 chicken thighs, skin on
1 teaspoon cumin, ground
1 teaspoon cinnamon, ground
½ smoked sweet paprika
2 red peppers, sliced into thin strips
1 large lemon, cut into 6 thick slices
1 handful green olives, stoned
1 cup (250 ml) gluten-free chicken stock or bone broth
4 pitted dates or dried apricots, chopped
1 small pinch of chili powder
5 ounces (150 grams) green beans, halved
1 handful fresh coriander, chopped
1 handful fresh parsley, chopped

Preparation
Sauté the onions with ghee in a suitable pan for 8 minutes until soft. Stir in spices, ginger and garlic then sauté for 1 minute. Add the skin-on chicken pieces

and cook until golden brown from both the sides. Stir in the olives, stock, dates lemon slices and red peppers. Cover and cook for 40 minutes on a simmer. Add the green beans and cook for 4 minutes. Garnish with almond, parsley, and coriander. Serve.

Moroccan Lamb Stew

Preparation time: 15 minutes
Cook time: 8 hours 42 minutes
Nutrition facts (per serving): 403 cal (13g fat, 27g protein, 2g fiber)

The classic Moroccan lamb stew is here to complete your Moroccan menu. This meal can be served on all special occasions and festive celebrations.

Ingredients (6 servings)
2 tablespoon olive oil
2 pounds (1 kilogram) diced lamb shoulder
2 onions, halved and sliced
5 garlic cloves, crushed
1 thumb-sized piece ginger, peeled and grated
1 tablespoon ground cumin
1 tablespoon ground coriander
1 teaspoon ground cinnamon
1 pinch saffron
½ large preserved lemon, zest, chopped
1 tablespoon honey
1 tablespoon tomato purée
2 1/4 cups (600 ml) hot beef stock
Zest and juice from 1 lemon
4 tablespoons (80 grams) pitted Kalamata olives
1 handful chopped mint
Couscous or rice, to serve

Preparation
Sauté the lamb meat with 1 tablespoon oil in a slow cooker on medium heat. Stir in the onions and more oil. Sauté for 10 minutes, add ginger and garlic, and sauté for 2 minutes. Next, add lemon, tomato puree, and spices. Add water and stock

and cover to cook for 8 hours on Low heat. Stir in the honey and olives. Cook for 30 minutes and serve with mint and couscous.

Tomato and Chickpea Soup with Couscous

Preparation time: 15 minutes
Cook time: 31 minutes
Nutrition facts (per serving): 341 cal (11g fat, 33g protein, 0g fiber)

This entrée is a staple for any festive celebration. This recipe will add a lot of appeal and color to your dinner table.

Ingredients (6 servings)
2 3/4 ounces (75 grams) couscous
3 tablespoon olive oil
3 cups (750 ml) low-sodium hot vegetable stock
1 large onion, chopped
1 carrot, chopped into small cubes
4 garlic cloves, crushed
Half a finger of ginger, peeled and chopped
1 tablespoon ras-el-hanout
1 tablespoon harissa paste
14 ounces (400 grams) tin chopped tomato
14 ounces (400 grams) tin chickpea
Juice ½ lemon
Chopped coriander, to serve

Preparation
Mix the couscous with salt, black pepper, and 1 tablespoon oil in a bowl. Pour in the hot stock and cover with cling film and then keep it aside. Sauté the onion and carrot with oil in a cooking pan for 8 minutes. Stir in ginger and garlic and then sauté for 2 minutes. Add harissa, ras el hanout, and cook for 1 minute. Add the stock, tomatoes, and chickpeas; then cover to cook for 20 minutes on a simmer. Add lemon juice and mix well. Serve the soup with couscous and garnish with coriander. Enjoy.

Chickpea, Squash, and Cavolo Nero Stew

Preparation time: 15 minutes
Cook time: 70 minutes
Nutrition facts (per serving): 378 cal (11g fat, 13g protein, 1.2g fiber)

The Moroccan Nero stew is here to complete your Moroccan menu. This meal can be served on all special occasions and memorable celebrations.

Ingredients (6 servings)

4 tomatoes, halved
5 tablespoon olive oil
9 ounces (250 grams) butternut squash, peeled and chopped into large chunks
1 tablespoon thyme leaves
1 garlic clove, crushed
1 onion, sliced
2 x 14 ounces (400 grams) cans chickpeas, drained
1 bay leaf
1 tablespoon ground cumin
1 teaspoon ground cinnamon
½ teaspoon turmeric
1 tablespoon harissa
4 cups (1 liter) vegetable stock
3 1/2 ounces (100 grams) feta, crumbled
1 lemon, zested, then cut into wedges
2 teaspoon fennel seeds
1 teaspoon ground coriander
7 ounces (200 grams) cavolo Nero, shredded
1 handful fresh coriander leaves, to serve

Preparation

At 390 degrees F, preheat your oven. Spread all the tomatoes on a suitable baking sheet lined with parchment paper and drizzle 2 tablespoon olive oil on top. Stir in the seasoning and roast in the oven for 20 minutes until soft. Meanwhile, sauté squash, with olive oil thyme, garlic and onion in a cooking pan for 15 minutes. Stir in the bay leaf, harissa, spices, chickpeas, stock and tomatoes. Cover and cook on a simmer for 30 minutes. Mix feta with lemon zest and remaining oil in a small bowl. Toast fennel seeds in a pan for 1 minute. Crush the seeds in a mortar. Add cavolo Nero and coriander to the stew. Cook for 2 minutes then top it with feta mixture. Garnish with fennel seeds and lemon wedges. Serve warm.

Sausage Stew

Preparation time: 10 minutes
Cook time: 27 minutes
Nutrition facts (per serving): 392 cal (19g fat, 25g protein, 2g fiber)

Sausage stew is here to add flavors to your dinner table, but this time with a mix of sausage, pitted dates, and tomato.

Ingredients (8 servings)
2 teaspoon vegetable oil
8 pork sausages
2 red onions, cut into wedges
1 garlic clove, crushed
2 tablespoon Moroccan spice mix or ras el hanout
3 1/2 ounces (100 grams) soft pitted dates, roughly chopped
14 ounces (400 grams) can chopped tomato
2/3 cup (175 ml) hot beef stock
1 tablespoon corn flour
Mashed potatoes, to serve

Preparation
Sauté the sausages and onions with oil in a casserole dish for 10 minutes, then add spice mix, garlic, then cook for 2 minutes. Stir in the tomatoes and dates, then add the stock and cover the lid for 10 minutes. Mix the corn flour with 2 tablespoon water and pour it into the stew and cook for 5 minutes with occasional stirring. Serve warm with mashed potatoes.

Roasted Vegetable Soup

Preparation time: 10 minutes
Cook time: 40 minutes
Nutrition facts (per serving): 471 cal (13g fat, 19g protein, 3g fiber)

Let's have a rich and delicious combination of roasted carrot, parsnip, butternut squash. Try it with warm bread slices, and you'll simply love it.

Ingredients (4 servings)
1 red onion, cut into 8 wedges
10 1/2 ounces (300grams) carrot, cut into 2/3 inch chunks
10 1/2 ounces (300grams) parsnip, cut into 2/3 inch chunks
10 1/2 ounces (300grams) peeled butternut squash, cut into 2/3 inch chunks
1 small potato, cut into 2/3 inch chunks
2 garlic cloves
1 tablespoon ras el hanout
1 ½ tablespoon olive oil
5 1/2 cups (1.3 liters) hot vegetable stock
6 tablespoon Greek-style yogurt and 1 tablespoon chopped mint, to serve

Preparation
At 390 degrees F, preheat your oven. Spread all the veggies and garlic in a roasting pan. Drizzle oil, ras el hanout, and seasoning on top, then roast them for 35 minutes while tossing halfway through. Transfer the roasted veggies to a saucepan and add the hot stock. Cook for 5 minutes, then puree the soup with a hand blender. Garnish with a dollop of yogurt, mint, and black pepper. Serve warm.

Quince Lamb Shanks Stew

Preparation time: 15 minutes
Cook time: 2 hours 51 minutes
Nutrition facts (per serving): 349 cal (3.6g fat, 22g protein, 5.4g fiber)

It's about time to try some classic lamb shanks stew on the menu and make it more diverse and flavorsome. Serve warm with your favorite herbs on top.

Ingredients (4 servings)
1 tablespoon olive oil
4 lamb shanks
1 large knob of butter
2 onions, cut into wedges
4 garlic cloves, crushed
4 strips zest and juice from 1 lemon
2 teaspoon ground cinnamon
2 teaspoon ground coriander
1 teaspoon ground ginger
1 teaspoon ground cumin
1 pinch of saffron strands
1 heaped tablespoon tomato purée
1 tablespoon clear honey
2 ½ cups (400 ml) beef stock
2 quinces, peeled, quartered and cored

Preparation
Sauté and sear the shanks with oil in a pan for 10 minutes until brown. At 350 degrees F, preheat your oven. Sauté the onion with melted butter in a cooking pan for 10 minutes, then add garlic. Add the spices and lemon zest, then sauté for 1 minute. Add the tomato puree, stock, lemon juice, and honey. Mix well, add lamb shank, and quince, cook the mixture to a simmer then, and bake for 2 hours in the oven. Remove its lid and bake for 30minutes. Transfer the lamb

and quinces to the serving plate. Cook the sauce until it thickens. Pour over the lam and garnish with lemon juice. Serve.

Lamb and Apricot Tagine

Preparation time: 10 minutes
Cook time: 7 hours 35 minutes
Nutrition facts (per serving): 472 cal (29g fat, 31g protein, 1.4g fiber)

Try this classic to make your meal special. You can always serve the tagine with your favorite rice or couscous.

Ingredients (4 servings)
1 large leg of lamb, bone-in (2kg)
21 ounces (600 grams) shallot, halved
14 ounces (400 grams) small apricot, halved and stoned
3 ounces (85 grams) whole skinless almond
2 preserved lemons, peel and chopped
1 tablespoon *ras el hanout*
1 tablespoon honey
2/3 cup (150 ml) hot chicken stock
1 small pack coriander, leaves picked
Couscous and natural yogurt, to serve

For the marinade
4 tablespoon olive oil
4 garlic cloves, crushed
1 tablespoon ground cumin
2 tablespoon honey
2 teaspoon ground cinnamon
2 teaspoon ground ginger
2 teaspoon coriander seed
Pinch of saffron strands

Preparation

Place the lamb leg in a casserole dish. Grind the marinade ingredients in a mortar with a pestle. Rub the mixture over the lamb leg, cover, and marinate for 24 hours in the refrigerator. At 325 degrees F, preheat your oven. Place the marinated lamb leg in a large roasting tin, cover it with a tin foil, and pinch the edges to seal. Roast the leg for 7 hours, basting with the marinade after every hour until the meat is tender. Remove the lamb from the leg and transfer the juices to a bowl. Add shallots to the lamb and roast for 15 minutes. Add apricot and almond on top. Mix the cooking juices with stock, honey, lemon, and ras el hanout in a bowl and pour over the lamb. Roast for another 20 minutes. Serve warm.

Moroccan Chicken One-Pot

Preparation time: 15 minutes
Cook time: 40 minutes
Nutrition facts (per serving): 373 cal (13g fat, 28g protein, 2g fiber)

This chicken one-pot tastes amazing, and it's simple and easy to cook. It's great for all chicken lovers.

Ingredients (4 servings)
4 chicken breasts, boneless, skinless
3 tablespoon olive oil
2 onions, 1 chopped, 1 sliced
3 1/2 ounces (100 grams) tomatoes, chopped
3 1/2 ounces (100 grams) ginger, roughly chopped
3 garlic cloves, chopped
1 teaspoon turmeric
1 tablespoon ground cumin
1 tablespoon coriander
1 tablespoon cinnamon
1 large butternut squash, deseeded and cubed
2 1/4 cups (600 ml) chicken stock
2 tablespoon brown sugar
2 tablespoon red wine vinegar
3 1/2 ounces (100 grams) dried cherries

To serve
1 small red onion, chopped
Zest 1 lemon
1 handful mint leaves
3 1/2 ounces (100 grams) feta cheese, crumbled
Couscous and natural yogurt

Preparation

Season the 4 chicken breasts with salt and black pepper. Sear them with 2 tablespoon oil in a dish until golden brown on both sides and then transfer to a plate. Finely chop the onion, tomatoes, ginger, and garlic in a food processor. Sauté the sliced onion with olive oil in a suitable pan until soft. Stir in the cumin, turmeric, cinnamon, and coriander, then sauté for 1 minute. Stir in the onion mixture. Add chicken, butternut squash, chicken stock, brown sugar, and red wine vinegar to the pan. Cook the mixture to a simmer and cook for 30 minutes. Stir in the dried cherries and cook until the sauce thickens. To serve, mix the red onion with lemon zest, mint leaves, and feta cheese in a bowl. Serve the chicken with an onion mixture on top.

Butternut Harissa Hummus

Preparation time: 15 minutes
Cook time: 40 minutes
Nutrition facts (per serving): 229 cal (14g fat, 14g protein, 14g fiber)

Harissa hummus is always an easy way to add extra fibers and nutrients to your menu, so try some that you can make in just a few minutes.

Ingredients (4 servings)
½ butternut squash (400 grams), peeled and diced
3 garlic cloves, unpeeled
2 tablespoon olive oil
3 tablespoon tahini paste
1 tablespoon harissa
14 ounces (400 grams) can chickpeas, drained and rinsed

Preparation
At 390 degrees F, preheat your oven. Spread squash and garlic in a roasting pan and add ¼ cup water. Cover the pan with a foil, bake for 45 minutes, and then allow it to cool. Transfer the squash to a blender, along with the juices, and then blend until smooth. Peel the garlic cloves and add them to the blender. Add the remaining ingredients and then blend until smooth. Serve.

Chicken Couscous with Dates

Preparation time: 15 minutes
Cook time: 35 minutes
Nutrition facts (per serving): 379 cal (13g fat, 25g protein, 3g fiber)

Here's a delicious and savory combination of chicken, cooked, and served with couscous and vegetables that you must add to your menu.

Ingredients (6 servings)
2 tablespoon olive oil
17 1/2 ounces (500 grams) skinless chicken thighs
5 ounces (140 grams) whole-wheat couscous
2 onions, sliced
4 garlic cloves, sliced
Zest 2 lemons, juice of 1
1 1/2 cups (150ml) chicken stock
1 teaspoon ground cumin
1 teaspoon ground cinnamon
6 large dates, pitted and chopped
1 2/3 ounces (50 grams) flaked almond
Small bunch parsley, chopped

Preparations
At 350 degrees F, preheat your oven. Sear the chicken with oil in a frying pan for 5 minutes per side until golden brown and then transfer to a baking dish with the couscous. Sauté the onions and garlic with remaining oil in the same pan for 5 minutes. Stir in lemon juice and zest, stock, dates, cinnamon, and cumin then cook to a boil. Pour this mixture over the chicken and drizzle almonds on top. Cover with a foil sheet and bake for 20 minutes. Garnish with parsley and zest.

Guinea Fowl Tagine

Preparation time: 15 minutes
Cook time: 1 hour 10 minutes
Nutrition facts (per serving): 336 cal (13g fat,28g protein, 1.7g fiber)

Here's a perfect mix of guinea fowl and butternut squash. Serve warm with your favorite side salad for the best taste.

Ingredients (8 servings)
3 tablespoon olive oil
2 guinea fowl, a chicken
2 onions, chopped
2 garlic cloves, chopped
1 butternut squash, peeled, deseeded, and diced
1 tablespoon ras-el-hanout
1 teaspoon ground cumin
1 teaspoon ground coriander
¼ teaspoon ground ginger
1 large cinnamon stick
1 teaspoon honey
1 large pinch of saffron, soaked in 1 tablespoon water
Juice 1 lemon
3 1/2 cups (850ml) chicken stock
14 ounces (400 grams) can chickpea, drained and rinsed
7 ounces (200 grams) dried apricot
1 small bunch of coriander
Couscous or rice, to serve

Preparation
Sauté the guinea fowl pieces with oil in a suitable casserole dish and transfer to a plate. Sauté the onions in the same dish until soft. Stir in the squash and garlic, then cook for 2 minutes. Add the spices, honey, lemon juice, saffron, stock, and

chickpeas. Return the guinea fowl pieces to the pan and add apricots. Cover and cook on a simmer for 1 hour. Garnish with coriander and serve warm with couscous.

Moroccan Meatball Tagine

Preparation time: 15 minutes
Cook time: 35 minutes
Nutrition facts (per serving): 316 cal (7g fat, 24g protein, 12g fiber)

The meatball tagine is famous for its unique taste and aroma, and now you can bring those exotic flavors home by using this recipe.

Ingredients (6 servings)
3 onions, peeled
17 1/2 ounces (500 grams) minced lamb
zest and juice of 1 lemon
1 teaspoon ground cumin
1 teaspoon ground cinnamon
1 pinch cayenne pepper
1 small bunch flat-leaf parsley, chopped
2 tablespoon olive oil
1 thumb-sized piece ginger, peeled and grated
1 red chili, deseeded and chopped
1 pinch of saffron strands
1 cup (250 ml) lamb stock
1 tablespoon tomato purée
3 1/2 ounces (100 grams) pitted black Kalamata olive
1 small bunch coriander, chopped
Couscous or fresh crusty bread, to serve

Preparation
Blend the onion in a food processor until chopped. Transfer half of the onion to a suitable bowl and add the lamb, spices, parsley, lemon zest, and mix well. Make walnut size meatballs out of this mixture. Sauté the remaining onions, ginger, saffron, and chilling in a casserole dish for 5 minutes then add stock, tomato puree, olives and lemon juice then cook to a boil. Stir in the meatballs

and cover to a cook for 20 minutes with occasional stirring. Remove its lid and cook for another 5 minutes. Garnish with lemon wedges and coriander. Serve warm.

Aromatic Lamb with Dates

Preparation time: 15 minutes
Cook time: 40 minutes
Nutrition facts (per serving): 386 cal (11g fat, 32g protein, 3g fiber)

This aromatic lamb with dates is a must-have for every fancy dinner. Thus, with the help of this recipe, you can cook them in no time.

Ingredients (2 servings)
1 tablespoon olive oil
1 onion, chopped
17 1/2 ounces (500 grams) diced boneless lamb
10 1/2 ounces (300 grams) sweet potatoes, diced
2 teaspoon ground coriander
2 teaspoon ground cinnamon
1 tablespoon tomato purée
1 2/3 ounces (50 grams) pitted dates
2 tablespoon coriander, roughly chopped

Preparation
Sauté the onion and lamb with oil in a pan until the lamb is brown. Stir in the sweet potatoes and spices and then toss well. Pour in boiling water and the tomato purée and cook to the boil. Cover and cook on a simmer for 15 minutes, add dates, and cook for another 10 minutes. Garnish with coriander and serve warm.

Pumpkin Cranberry Tagine

Preparation time: 15 minutes
Cook time: 25 minutes
Nutrition facts (per serving): 428 cal (17g fat, 11g protein, 8g fiber)

The refreshing pumpkin tagine always tastes great when you cook pumpkin and cranberry, all together with harissa paste and passata.

Ingredients (6 servings)
3 tablespoon olive oil
2 red onions, thickly sliced
1 inch piece fresh root ginger, grated
1-pound (500 grams) pumpkin, peeled, deseeded, and diced
1 teaspoon cinnamon
1 teaspoon coriander
1 teaspoon cumin
1 teaspoon harissa paste
1 tablespoon honey
1 1/2 pounds (700 grams) bottle tomato passata
1 2/3 ounces (50 grams) dried cranberries
14 ounces (400 grams) can chickpea, rinsed and drained
7 ounces (200 grams) couscous
2 teaspoon vegetable stock granules
Zest and juice 1 lemon
3 tablespoon toasted flaked almonds
1 handful coriander, roughly chopped

Preparation
Sauté the onions with 2 tablespoon oil in a suitable pan until golden. Stir in ginger, spices, honey, pumpkin, cranberries, and passata, then cook to a boil. Reduce its heat, cover to a cook on a simmer for 20 minutes, and add chickpeas after 10 minutes. Meanwhile, mix the couscous with lemon zest, hot water, and

stock granules in a suitable bowl, cover, and leave for 5 minutes. Stir in the lemon juice, almond, and remaining oil then mix well. Serve the cooked pumpkin tagine with couscous. Enjoy.

Moroccan Spiced Fish with Ginger Mash

Preparation time: 15 minutes
Cook time: 18 minutes
Nutrition facts (per serving): 342 cal (17g fat, 38g protein, 0g fiber)

Are you in a mood to have sweet potatoes and white fish fillets on the menu? Well, you can with this spiced fish with sweet potato ginger mash.

Ingredients (4 servings)
2 sweet potatoes, peeled and diced
2 teaspoon butter, softened
1 garlic clove, crushed
1 teaspoon harissa
Zest 1 lemon
1 small handful coriander, chopped
1 fingertip-size ginger, grated
2 skinless white fish fillets

Preparation
At 350 degrees F, preheat your oven. Add all the sweet potatoes with a pinch of salt to boiling water and cook for 10 minutes until soft, then drain. Mix the butter with harissa, garlic, lemon zest, seasoning, and coriander in a bowl. Keep half of the butter mixture aside and add sweet potatoes to the remaining mixture and mash with a fork. Mix well and keep it aside. Place the white fish fillets in a baking pan and brush them with the reserved butter mixture. Bake the fish for 8 minutes then serve with sweet potato mash. Enjoy.

Moroccan Meatballs

Preparation time: 10 minutes
Cook time: 30 minutes
Nutrition facts (per serving): 425 cal (28g fat, 33g protein, 2g fiber)

Have you tried the Moroccan meatballs before? Well, now you can enjoy this unique and flavorsome combination by cooking this recipe at home.

Ingredients (8 servings)
1 tablespoon olive oil
3 pack beef meatballs
1 large onion, sliced
3 1/2 ounces (100 grams) dried apricot, halved
1 small cinnamon stick
14 ounces (400 grams) tin chopped tomato with garlic
1 tablespoon toasted flaked almond
1 handful coriander, roughly chopped

Preparation
Sauté the meatballs with oil in a pan for 10 minutes transfer to a plate. Add onion and sauté for 5 minutes. Stir in the cinnamon stick, tomatoes, half a can of water, and apricots and cook for 10 minutes on a simmer then remove the cinnamon stick. Return the seared meatballs to the pan along with the tomato sauce. Mix and cook for almost 5 minutes and then garnish with coriander and almonds. Serve warm.

Moroccan Roast Lamb with Roasted Roots

Preparation time: 15 minutes
Cook time: 60 minutes
Nutrition facts (per serving): 443 cal (16g fat, 23g protein, 0.6g fiber)

Moroccan roast lamb is always served as a complete meal, and this one, in particular, is great to have on a nutritious diet.

Ingredients (6 servings)
½ leg (800 grams) of lamb
2 red onions, chopped
1 butternut squash, skin left on, chopped
1 celeriac, peeled and chopped
2½ tablespoon cold-pressed rapeseed oil
2 tablespoon ras el hanout
8 garlic cloves, skin on
1 small bunch of coriander
½ teaspoon cumin seeds
1 lemon, zested and juiced
1⁄2 green chili, deseeded

Preparation
At 390 degrees F, preheat your oven. Cut a few slits on top of the lamb leg and rub it with ½ tablespoon oil and 1 tablespoon ras el hanout, salt, and black pepper. Toss the onion with butternut squash and celeriac with remaining oil, salt, black pepper, ras el hanout, and garlic. Place the lamb leg on top and roast for 40 minutes. Remove the lamb from the pan and return the veggies for 20 minutes. Blend coriander, lemon juice, lemon zest, cumin seeds and green chili in a mini blender. Place the lamb in the serving plate, slice it, add roasted veggies, and coriander mixture on top. Serve warm.

Moroccan Spiced Pie

Preparation time: 10 minutes
Cook time: 40 minutes
Nutrition facts (per serving): 478 cal (16g fat, 24g protein, 2g fiber)

This Moroccan spiced pie tastes heavenly when cooked with squash and shallots filling. Serve warm with your favorite salads on the side.

Ingredients (6 servings)

2 teaspoons coriander seeds
2 teaspoons cumin
1 teaspoon paprika
½ teaspoon ground cinnamon
11/4 cup (50 ml) olive oil
32 ounces (900 grams) squash, peeled and diced
12 shallots, quartered
1½ in piece root ginger, chopped
5 ounces (140 grams) whole blanched almonds
5 ounces (140 grams) shelled pistachios
2 3/4 ounces (75 grams) pack dried cranberries
6 tablespoon honey
8 ounces (225 grams) pack fresh spinach
14 ounces (400 grams) can chickpeas, drained and rinsed
2 garlic cloves
1 teaspoon ground cumin
3 tablespoon lemon juice
4 tablespoon chopped fresh coriander
3 1/2 ounces (100 grams) butter
8 large sheets of filo pastry
Lemon wedges to serve

For the harissa yogurt sauce
7 ounces (200 grams) carton Greek yogurt
6 tablespoon milk
3 large sprigs mint, leaves chopped
2-3 tablespoon harissa paste

Preparation

At 350 degrees F, preheat your oven. Toast all the seeds in a suitable frying pan until golden then transfer to a mortar and grind with a pestle. Add 4 tablespoons oil, ½ teaspoon salt, cinnamon, and paprika then mix well. Toss the squash with spiced oil in a roasting pan and roast for 20 minutes. Sauté the shallots with 2 tablespoons oil in a frying pan until brown. Add almonds, pistachios, and ginger. Stir in 2 tablespoons honey, spinach, and cranberries. Add this mixture to the squash.

Blend the chickpeas with remaining oil, cumin, garlic, 2 tablespoons water, black pepper, salt, and lemon juice in a blender. Add coriander and mix well. Melt butter and brush a quiche pan with this melted butter. Spread one sheet at the bottom of the pan and add another layer of the sheet. Brush again with melted. Continue adding more phyllo sheets in the same way to get eight layers. Add half of the squash filling and top it with hummus. Spread the remaining squash filling on top and cover with the remaining phyllo sheet and butter. Bake the pie for 35 minutes in the oven. Brush honey on top. Blend the harissa yogurt sauce in a blender. Serve the pie with the sauce and enjoy it.

Spiced Bulgur Wheat with Roasted Peppers

Preparation time: 15 minutes
Cook time: 4 minutes
Nutrition facts (per serving): 338 cal (10g fat, 13g protein, 3g fiber)

Now you can quickly make flavorsome spiced bulgur wheat with roasted peppers and serve them to have a fancy meal for yourself and your guest.

Ingredients (6 servings)
7 ounces (200 grams) bulgur wheat
1 cup (250 ml) hot vegetable stock
½ teaspoon Moroccan spice mix
Zest 1 lemon, juice of ½ lemon
1 tablespoon olive oil
½ red onion, finely sliced
14 ounces (400 grams) can chickpea, drained
7 1/2 ounces (210 grams) jar roasted pepper, drained
1 small bunch of coriander, leaves only

Preparation
Add bulgur wheat and stock to a bowl, cover with a cling film, and then heat for 4 minutes on high heat in a microwave. Keep it aside for 5 minutes. Mix the remaining spices, olive oil, and lemon zest in a salad bowl. Toss in onion, pepper, chickpea, coriander, and peppers. Stir in bulgur wheat and then mix well. Serve.

Spicy Moroccan Rice

Preparation time: 10 minutes
Cook time: 20 minutes
Nutrition facts (per serving): 321 cal (10g fat, 24g protein, g fiber)

Spicy Moroccan rice is always a delight on a menu. Now you can make it easily at home by using the following simple ingredients.

Ingredients (4 servings)
4 skinless chicken breasts, diced
1 tablespoon Moroccan spice seasoning
1 onion, finely sliced
1 2/3 ounces (50 grams) butter
10 1/2 ounces (300 grams) rice
12 dried apricots, halved
1 chicken stock cube
15 ounces (410 grams) can chickpeas, drained and rinsed
2 tablespoons of flatleaf parsley, chopped

Preparation
Rub the chicken with Moroccan spice. Sauté an onion with butter in a pan until soft. Add chicken and cook until golden brown. Stir in the apricots, rice, chickpeas, and boiling water. Cover this pan and cook for 10 minutes until the liquid is absorbed. Garnish with parsley. Serve warm.

Moroccan Freekeh Traybake

Preparation time: 10 minutes
Cook time: 30 minutes
Nutrition facts (per serving): 278 cal (11g fat, 25g protein, 3g fiber)

If you haven't tried the Moroccan *Freekeh Traybake* before, then here comes a simple and easy to cook a recipe that you can recreate at home swiftly.

Ingredients (8 servings)
2 tablespoon olive oil
14 ounces (400 grams) can chickpeas, rinsed, and drained
1 teaspoon ground coriander
1 teaspoon ground cumin
½ teaspoon chili flakes
9 1/2 ounces (270 grams) cherry tomatoes
½ x 14 ounces (400 grams) can apricot halves, drained and roughly chopped
2 1/2 ounces (70 grams) green olives
9 ounces (250 grams) pouch cooked freekeh
2 1/2 ounces (70 grams) fat-free Greek yogurt
1 small bunch dill, chopped

Preparation
At 350 degrees F, preheat your oven. Toss the chickpeas with chili flakes and spices in a roasting pan and roast for 15 minutes until golden. Stir in apricots, tomatoes, freekeh, and olive then toss. Roast for 15 minutes. Blend the yogurt with salt and dill. Serve freekeh bake with herbed yogurt. Enjoy.

Moroccan Roast Chicken with Apricots

Preparation time: 10 minutes
Cook time: 50 minutes
Nutrition facts (per serving): 391 cal (7g fat, 27g protein, 2g fiber)

Try seasoning the chicken with some unique combination of spices and cook it with a blend of apricot to enjoy the best of Moroccan cuisine.

Ingredients (10 servings)
2 small chicken
6 tablespoon olive oil
1 small bunch coriander
2 tablespoon sumacs
1 tablespoon cumin seed
1 tablespoon fennel seed
2 teaspoon chili flakes
2 garlic cloves
Zest and juice 2 lemons
4 tablespoon pomegranate molasses
9 ounces (250 grams) natural yogurt

For the apricots
12 apricots, halved and stoned
2 preserved lemons, rinsed, seeds removed, chopped
3 tablespoon honey
1 tablespoon orange blossom water
4 tablespoon white wine vinegar

Preparation
Blend olive oil, sumac, coriander, garlic, lemon zest, lemon juice, cumin, fennel, chili, black pepper, and pomegranate molasses in a blender to make a paste. Divide this mixture into two Ziplock bags, divide the chicken in these bags, seal,

and keep in the refrigerator for 48 hours approximately. At 375 degrees F, preheat your oven. roast the chicken for 30 minutes in the oven. Add apricots to a roasting pan. Mix the preserved lemon, orange blossom, vinegar and honey in a bowl then pour it over the apricots. Roast them for 20 minutes. Serve warm around the chicken.

Lentils and Pasta With Tamarind

Preparation time: 10 minutes
Cook time: 41 minutes
Nutrition facts (per serving): 396 cal (13g fat, 12g protein, 4g fiber)

Lentils with pasta are loved by all, the old and the young, and they make a healthy meal. Try this recipe to make some.

Ingredients (8 servings)
1-ounce tamarind, soaked in 2/3 cup (200 ml) boiling water
9 ounces (250 grams) fettuccini, broken up roughly
2 tablespoons olive oil
2 red onions, thinly sliced (around 350 grams)
6 cups (1 ½ liter) chicken stock
12 ounces (350 grams) brown lentils
2 tablespoon pomegranate molasses
Sea salt flakes
Black pepper
6 garlic cloves, crushed
1-ounce (30 grams) coriander, roughly chopped
2/3 ounces (20 grams) parsley, roughly chopped
3 ounces (90 grams) pomegranate seeds
2 teaspoon sumacs
2 lemons, cut into wedges

Preparation
Soak the tamarind in water in a bowl for 10 minutes, then strain its liquid and remove the pips. Keep this liquid aside. Add fettuccine to a saucepan and toast them for 2 minutes. Sauté onion with 2 tablespoon oil in a cooking pan for 8 minutes until golden. Add chicken stock, lentils, and cook for 20 minutes. Stir in the tamarind water, toasted fettuccine, water pomegranate molasses, black pepper, and 4 teaspoon salt. Cook for 9 minutes. Meanwhile, sauté the garlic

with 2 tablespoon oil in a pan until golden brown. Add garlic to the pasta and garnish with the remaining ingredients. Serve warm.

Chicken Tagine

Preparation time: 10 minutes
Cook time: 53 minutes
Nutrition facts (per serving): 492 cal (13g fat, 39g protein, 0.5g fiber)

This one-pot chicken tagine is a flavorsome mix of chicken with harissa, which is cooked and served with couscous and herbs.

Ingredients (4 servings)
4 boneless chicken breasts
1 tablespoon harissa paste
1 large onion, sliced
1 Knorr Chicken stock cube
3 1/2 ounces (100 grams) dried apricots, halved
14 ounces (400 grams) can chopped tomatoes
Couscous to serve, optional
Herbs to garnish, optional

Preparation
Season the chicken with harissa paste. Sear chicken in 1 tablespoon olive oil in a large pan for 3 minutes. Then transfer to a plate. Add the onion to the same pan and sauté for 5 minutes, then return the chicken to the pan. Stir in the tomatoes, apricots, and stock then cover and cook for 45 minutes on low heat. Serve warm with herbs and couscous.

Fruity Lamb Tagine

Preparation time: 10 minutes
Cook time: 1 hour 3 minutes
Nutrition facts (per serving): 408 cal (10g fat, 34g protein, 0.4g fiber)

If you want something exotic on your dinner table, then nothing can taste better than this spiced, fruity lamb tagine.

Ingredients (6 servings)

21 ounces (600 grams) diced lamb steaks
3-4 tablespoons Ras el Hanout spice mix
1 large onion, diced
2-3 garlic cloves, finely sliced
1 tablespoon runny honey
1 Knorr stock cube dissolved in 3 ½ cups boiling water
3 1/2 ounces (100 grams) dried apricots, halved
14 ounces (400 grams) can chopped tomatoes
Couscous to serve, optional
A handful of coriander and mint leaves, roughly chopped, optional

Preparation

Mix the lamb with half of the spice mix in a bowl, cover, and marinate for 30 minutes. Sear lamb steaks in 1 tablespoon oil in a large pan until brown from all the sides. Transfer them to a plate. Add the onion and sliced garlic to the same pan. Stir in the remaining spice mix and sauté for 3 minutes. Add the tomatoes, apricots, tomatoes, stock, and honey, cover, and cook for 1 hour on a simmer. Garnish with herbs and serve warm.

Chermoula Lamb Leg Steaks

Preparation time: 10 minutes
Cook time: 8 minutes
Nutrition facts (per serving): 457 cal (19g fat, 23g protein, 5g fiber)

Chermoula lamb leg steaks are one delicious way to complete your Moroccan menu; here's a recipe that you can try to have a tasty meal.

Ingredients (4 servings)

Chermoula
2 Pinch of saffron
1½ tablespoon lemon juice
1 teaspoon finely grated lemon zest
½ bunch of fresh coriander, shredded
2 garlic cloves, peeled and crushed
½ tablespoon paprika
½ tablespoon lightly toasted cumin seeds
Pinch of ground ginger
Generous pinch of flaky sea salt
Olive oil

For the lamb
4 lamb leg steaks (300 grams)
1 pinch of chermoula
½ cucumber, grated
½ teaspoon coarse salt
A small handful of mint leaves
2/3 cup (200 ml) Greek yogurt
2 tablespoons olive oil

Preparation

Mix the saffron with lemon zest and juice in a bowl and leave for 10 minutes. Add the remaining chermoula ingredients and mix well. Mix the steaks with half of the chermoula and cover to refrigerate for 2 hours. Mix the cucumber with salt in a suitable colander and leave for 30 minutes. Drain and rinse the cucumber. Mix the cucumber with shredded mint leaves, seasoning, olive oil, and yogurt in a bowl. Remove the lamb leg steaks from the marinade and sear them with oil for 4 minutes per side in a pan. Serve warm with mint yogurt.

Spiced Lamb and Herby Quinoa

Preparation time: 10 minutes
Cook time: 60 minutes
Nutrition facts (per serving): 424 cal (16g fat, 19g protein, 14g fiber)

Let's make spiced lamb with herby quinoa with these simple ingredients. Mix them together and then cook to have great flavors.

Ingredients (6 servings)
17 1/2 ounces (500 grams) lean lamb mince
1 tablespoon light olive oil
1 red onion, chopped
2 tablespoon plain flour
2 teaspoon ground cumin
2 teaspoon ground coriander
½ teaspoon ground cinnamon
1-2 green chilies, chopped
2 inch piece fresh ginger, grated
2 fat garlic cloves, crushed
2 cups (500 ml) fresh chicken or lamb stock
2/3 cup (200 ml) tomato passata
Seeds ½ pomegranate

For the herby quinoa
13 ounces (90 grams) quinoa, cooked
2 tablespoon extra-virgin olive oil
5 ounces (150 grams) feta, crumbled
Zest 1 lemon
A handful of fresh mint leaves sliced
Handful fresh parsley leaves chopped

Preparation

Sauté the lamb mince in a pan until brown then transfer to a colander. Add oil to the same pan and sauté the onion for 10 minutes on low heat. Stir in spices, ginger, garlic, chilies, and flour, then sauté for 2 minutes approximately. Add the lamb mince to the pan and pour in passata and stock. Cook the mixture to a boil then reduce its heat. Cook for 30 minutes on a simmer until the sauce thickens. Mix the quinoa with olive oil, feta, herbs, and lemon zest in a bowl. Spread the lamb mixture in a baking dish and top it with a quinoa mixture. Bake it for 25 minutes in the oven at 360 degrees F. Serve warm with herbs on top. Enjoy.

Grilled Mackerel with Pesto Freekeh Salad

Preparation time: 10 minutes
Cook time: 37 minutes
Nutrition facts (per serving): 359 cal (5 g fat, 33g protein, 1g fiber)

Count on this recipe to make your dinner extra special and surprise your loved one with the ultimate flavors.

Ingredients (8 servings)
Olive oil for frying
1 red onion, chopped
1 tablespoon balsamic vinegar
7 ounces (200 grams) freekeh
2 cups (500 ml) chicken stock
1 squeeze lemon juice
8 skin-on mackerel fillets
3 large pink grapefruit, segmented and juice reserved
3 1/2 ounces (100 grams) young leaf spinach
1 tablespoon fresh flatleaf parsley, chopped

For the pesto
3 1/2 ounces (100 grams) pine nuts, toasted
1 2/3 ounces (50 grams) basil
1 2/3 ounces (50 grams) fresh flatleaf parsley
1/2 cup (120 ml) extra-virgin olive oil
1 2/3 ounces (50 grams) parmesan, grated
Reserved juice from the grapefruit

Preparation
Sauté the onion with oil in a large suitable pan for 6 minutes. Stir in freekeh, and balsamic vinegar, then cook for 3 minutes. Stir in the stock and cook for 20 minutes on a simmer. Remove the pan from the heat and allow the mixture to

cool. Blend half of the pine nuts with the pesto ingredients in a blender until smooth. Rub the mackerel fillets with lemon juice and olive oil. Preheat and prepare a grill. Grill the mackerel fish for 4 minutes per side. Mix half of the pesto with freekeh, parsley, spinach, and grapefruit in a serving dish. Place the grilled fish on top and garnish with pine nuts and remaining pesto. Serve.

Chicken Basteeya

Preparation time: 10 minutes
Cook time: 88 minutes
Nutrition facts (per serving): 482 cal (13g fat, 29g protein, 6g fiber)

This Chicken *Basteeya* will melt your heart away with its epic flavors. This chicken pie is filled with an almond mixed chicken filling that you can easy cook and savor.

Ingredients (8 servings)
4 ounces (125 grams) unsalted butter
8 chicken thighs
2 onions, finely sliced
5 garlic cloves, crushed
Large thumb-size piece fresh ginger, finely grated
½ teaspoon ground turmeric
2 teaspoon ground coriander
1 teaspoon ground cumin
½ teaspoon paprika
1 teaspoon ground cinnamon
3 1/2 ounces (100 grams) blanched almonds, chopped
2 tablespoon icing sugar, plus extra
1 2/3 ounces (50 grams) sultanas
Zest 1 lemon and juice ½
3 medium free-range eggs, beaten
Small bunch fresh flatleaf parsley, leaves roughly chopped
Small bunch fresh coriander, roughly chopped
5-6 filo pastry sheets

Preparation
Add 2/3-ounce butter to a large deep-frying pan and melt over medium heat. Add chicken and sear for almost 3 minutes per side. Drizzle salt on top for

seasoning. Transfer the chicken to a plate. Add onion and sauté for 6 minutes. Stir in ginger and garlic, then sauté for 2 minutes. Add spices and cook for 4 minutes. Return the seared chicken pieces to the pan and pour in water. Partially cover and cook for 30 minutes on a simmer.

Transfer the chicken to a plate. Cook the liquid for 10 minutes until it thickens. Remove it from the heat and allow it to cool. Stir in the sugar, almonds, sultanas, lemon zest, and lemon juice. Stir in eggs and mix well. Transfer the sauce to a large bowl. Remove the cooked chicken from its bones and shred it with a fork. Return the meat to the sauce. Stir in the herbs, mix well, and then allow it to cool. Melt the remaining butter in a skillet and brush it in a cake pan. Spread one filo sheet in the pan and brush it with butter then add another layer of the sheet. Add the chicken filling, place the 2 filo sheets on top, and finally brush the butter on top. Bake for 30 minutes in the oven. Garnish with cinnamon and sugar. Serve warm.

Moroccan Roasted Vegetables with Couscous

Preparation time: 10 minutes
Cook time: 50 minutes
Nutrition facts (per serving): 381 cal (17g fat, 7g protein, 1g fiber)

If you haven't tried the Moroccan veggies with couscous before, then here comes a simple and easy to recreate at home in no time.

Ingredients (4 servings)
2 parsnips (200 grams), peeled and quartered
14 ounces (400 grams) chantenay carrots, trimmed
1 small or ½ large cauliflower (500 grams), florets
4 garlic cloves, unpeeled
2 teaspoon ras el hanout
2 tablespoon honey
4 tablespoon olive oil
7 ounces (200 grams) couscous
1 cup (250 ml) vegetable stock, hot
Juice of ½ lemon

Preparation
At 390 degrees F, preheat your oven. Layer a baking tray with parchment paper. Toss the vegetables, garlic, and ras el hanout in a baking tray. Drizzle olive oil and honey on top. Roast them for 45 minutes until caramelized. Add 1 tablespoon oil and couscous to a bowl and pour in the hot stock. Cover and leave for 5 minutes. Fluff the couscous. Add lemon juice and remaining oil. Divide the couscous on top of the veggies. Garnish with yogurt and coriander leaves. Serve warm.

Zigni Berbere

Preparation time: 15 minutes
Cook time: 1 hour 40 minutes
Nutrition facts (per serving): 412 cal (9g fat, 31g protein, 0.5g fiber)

The famous *Zigni berbere* recipe is here to make your Moroccan cuisine extra special. Make it with chicken and flatbreads for the best taste.

Ingredients (6 servings)
1/4 cup (50 ml) vegetable oil
2 large onions, chopped
4 garlic cloves, crushed
2 pounds (1 kg) chicken thighs, boneless, cut into cubes
2 x 14 ounces (400 grams) tins plum tomatoes
2 beef stock cubes
1 tablespoon tomato paste
½ cup (125 ml) dry red wine
1 bundle fresh coriander, chopped, to serve
Flatbreads to serve

For the berbere pepper blend
1 teaspoon ground ginger
1 teaspoon fenugreek
1 teaspoon black pepper
½ teaspoon ground coriander
½ teaspoon ground cardamom
¼ teaspoon ground cloves
¼ teaspoon ground allspice
Pinch ground cinnamon
½ tablespoon fine sea salt
1 tablespoon mild paprika

Preparation

Sauté the onions with oil in a large pan for 5 minutes until golden. Stir in garlic and sauté for 3 minutes. Mix all the berbere ingredients in a small bowl and keep it aside. Add the chicken and onions to the pan and sauté until golden. Stir in the remaining ingredients, along with berbere blend, and then cook for 1 ½ hour on a simmer. Serve warm.

Beef Daube

Preparation time: 10 minutes
Cook time: 1 hour 33 minutes
Nutrition facts (per serving): 470 cal (12g fat, 24g protein,6 g fiber)

This Moroccan beef *daube* has unique flavors due to its rich blend of stew meat with butternut squash. Serve warm with yellow rice and herbed yogurt.

Ingredients (6 servings)
2 tablespoon all-purpose flour
1 1/2 teaspoon salt
1 teaspoon ground cumin
1 teaspoon ground coriander
1 teaspoon ground cinnamon
1 teaspoon ground turmeric
2-pound beef stew meat
4 tablespoon olive oil
1 cup chopped butternut squash
1/2 red onion, chopped
2 garlic cloves, smashed
2 cups beef stock
1 (14.5-ounces) can diced tomatoes
1 tablespoon sherry vinegar
1 bay leaf
4 cups cooked yellow rice

Herby Yogurt
1 cup Greek yogurt
1/4 cup fresh mixed herbs, chopped
1 teaspoon orange zest
2 Tablespoon fresh juice
1/2 teaspoon salt

Preparation

Mix salt, flour, cumin, cinnamon, coriander, and turmeric in a small bowl. Rub this spice mixture on the stew meat and sear the meat in 2 tablespoon oil in a cooking pan for 5 minutes per side in a Dutch oven in batches. Transfer the meat to a plate. Add the onion, garlic, and squash; then sauté for 3 minutes. Add the stock, vinegar, bay leaf, and tomatoes, then cook to a simmer. Add meat and cook for 1 hour and 20 minutes on medium-low heat. Meanwhile, mix all the herby yogurt ingredients in a bowl. Serve the beef daube with yogurt on top. Serve warm.

Spiced Roasted Chicken with Sweet Onions

Preparation time: 15 minutes
Cook time: 20 minutes
Nutrition facts (per serving): 456 cal (15g fat, 26g protein, 0.7g fiber)

The roast chicken with sweet onions tastes great and makes an interesting combination with ras el hanout.

Ingredients (4 servings)
1 tablespoon olive oil
1 tablespoon ras el hanout
4 (6-ounce) skinless, boneless chicken breast halves
1/4 teaspoon salt
Cooking spray
1 tablespoon butter
2 cups sliced yellow onion
1/4 teaspoon salt
2 teaspoons honey
Lemon wedges

Preparation
Sauté the oil with ras el hanout in a skillet for 3 minutes. Add chicken breast and toasted spice mixture to a sealable bag. Seal this bag and shake well to coat well. Marinate the chicken for 10 minutes. Remove the chicken from the bag and season the chicken with ¼ teaspoon salt. At 350 degrees F, preheat your oven. Grease a skillet with cooking spray. Sear the boneless chicken for 4 minutes per side, and then remove from the pan. Add the butter, onion, and ¼ teaspoon salt, then sauté for 2 minutes. Return the cooked and seared chicken to the pan and stir in honey. Bake for 10 minutes at approximately 350 degrees F. Garnish with lemon wedges. Serve warm.

Grilled Eggplant with Moroccan Spices

Preparation time: 15 minutes
Cook time: 15 minutes
Nutrition facts (per serving): 319cal (14g fat, 9g protein, 7g fiber)

Grilled eggplant with Moroccan spices is one option for dinner. Sure, it takes some time to get it ready, but its great taste is definitely worth all the time and effort.

Ingredients (6 servings)
1 teaspoon coriander seeds
1 teaspoon cumin seeds
1/2 teaspoon freshly ground black pepper
Dash of ground red pepper
Dash of ground cinnamon
3/4 cup plain low-fat yogurt
2 tablespoons olive oil
1 tablespoon chopped fresh mint
1 tablespoon chopped fresh flat-leaf parsley
2 (1-pound) eggplants
Cooking spray
3/8 teaspoon salt

Preparation
At medium heat, preheat your grill and grease the grates with oil. Toast cumin and coriander in a suitable skillet over medium heat for 1 minute until golden. Transfer to a mortar and add black pepper, red pepper, and cinnamon, then crush with a pestle. Mix ½ teaspoon of this spice mixture with mint, oil, parsley, and yogurt in a bowl. Peel the eggplant with a vegetable peeler lengthwise. Slice the eggplant into ½ inch thick slices. Rub the eggplant slices with oil and season with the remaining spice mixture. Grill the slices for 5 minutes per side. Transfer the eggplant to a platter and pour over the yogurt on top. Cover with a foil sheet

and then leave it for 1 hour. Garnish with 1 tablespoon oil and a drizzle of salt. Serve.

Moroccan Lamb, Chickpea Burgers

Preparation time: 5 minutes
Cook time: 16 minutes
Nutrition facts (per serving): 376 cal (14g fat, 22g protein, 18g fiber)

This Moroccan lamb burger recipe will make your day with its delightful taste. Serve warm with your favorite bread and salad.

Ingredients (6 servings)
15 ounces (410 grams) tin chickpeas, drained and rinsed
2 carrots, coarsely grated
2 garlic cloves, crushed
2 teaspoon ras el hanout
1 teaspoon ground cumin
1 red chili, deseeded and chopped
1 medium egg
1 large handful of fresh coriander, chopped
5 ounces (150 grams) lamb mince
2 tablespoon olive oil
A squeeze of lemon juice
Flour for dusting

Preparation
Mix half of the carrots, chickpeas, garlic, dried spices, egg, chili, and coriander in a bowl. Blend half of this chickpea mixture in a blender until smooth. Add this blend to a bowl, add the reserved chickpea mixture and lamb, then mix well. Make 8 small burgers from this mixture. Place the patties on a plate and cover to refrigerate for 15 minutes. Mix the remaining carrots with coriander, 1 tablespoon oil, and lemon juice in a bowl. Add the remaining oil to a suitable pan and heat over medium heat. Lightly coat the burgers with flour and sear them for 4 minutes per side in the hot oil. Serve warm with carrot salad. Enjoy.

Fish Tagine

Preparation time: 15 minutes
Cook time: 21 minutes
Nutrition facts (per serving): 349 cal (7g fat, 29g protein, 3g fiber)

If you want some new flavors in your meals, then this fish tagine recipe is best to bring variety to the menu.

Ingredients (4 servings)
4 x 5 ounces (150 grams) skinless cod fillets
17 1/2 ounces (500 grams) potatoes
4 garlic cloves, chopped
3 tablespoon olive oil
2 green peppers, sliced
1 yellow pepper, sliced
5 tomatoes, roughly chopped
1/4 cup (100 ml) vegetable stock
3 1/2 ounces (100 grams) pitted green olives
Lemon wedges and fresh coriander, to garnish

For the marinade
2 teaspoon ground cumin
1 teaspoon ground coriander
4 tablespoon lemon juice
2 large garlic cloves
1 small bunch fresh coriander
1 teaspoon salt

Preparation
Blend all the fish marinade ingredients in a mini blender, rub it over the cod, and cover to refrigerate for 20 minutes. Meanwhile, boil all the potatoes in salted water until soft, then drain and slice in half. Sauté garlic with oil in a frying pan

for 2 minutes. Stir in the peppers and sauté for 5 minutes. Stir in the chopped tomatoes and cook for 2 minutes. Stir the remaining marinade and stock. Add the potatoes, half of the tomato mixture, and fish. Next, top with the remaining tomato mixture. Spread olive on top, cover, and cook for 12 minutes on medium-high heat. Garnish with coriander and lemon wedge. Serve warm.

Chicken Marrakesh

Preparation time: 15 minutes
Cook time: 4 hours
Nutrition facts (per serving): 411 cal (12g fat, 28g protein, 7g fiber)

When you can't think of anything to serve in the lunch or dinner, then this chicken Marrakesh will help you big time.

Ingredients (6 servings)
3/4 onion, sliced
1-1/2 garlic cloves, minced
1-1/2 large carrots, peeled and diced
1-1/2 large sweet potatoes, peeled and diced
3/4 (15 ounces) can garbanzo beans, drained and rinsed
1-1/2 pounds skinless, boneless chicken breast halves, cut into 2-inch pieces
1/4 teaspoon ground cumin
1/8 teaspoon ground turmeric
1/8 teaspoon ground cinnamon
1/4 teaspoon ground black pepper
3/4 teaspoon dried parsley
3/4 teaspoon salt
3/4 (14.5 ounces) can diced tomatoes

Preparation
Toss the sweet potato with garbanzo beans, chicken breasts, carrots, and onion in a slow cooker. Mix the turmeric, cinnamon, cumin, black pepper, parsley, and salt in a suitable bowl and drizzle over the chicken. Add the tomatoes and mix well. Cover to cook for 4 hours on high heat. Serve warm.

Marrakesh Vegetable Curry

Preparation time: 10 minutes
Cook time: 33 minutes
Nutrition facts (per serving): 326 cal (17g fat, 14g protein, 1.2g fiber)

Here's another classic recipe for your dinner or lunch recipe collection. Serve it with a tangy side salad and enjoy the best of it.

Ingredients (6 servings)
1 sweet potato, peeled and cubed
1 medium eggplant, cubed
1 green bell pepper, chopped
1 red bell pepper, chopped
2 carrots, chopped
1 onion, chopped
6 tablespoons olive oil
3 garlic cloves, minced
1 teaspoon ground turmeric
1 tablespoon curry powder
1 teaspoon ground cinnamon
¾ tablespoon of sea salt
¾ teaspoon cayenne pepper
1 (15 ounces) can garbanzo beans, drained
¼ cup blanched almonds
1 zucchini, sliced
2 tablespoons raisins
1 cup of orange juice
10 ounces spinach

Preparation
Sauté the sweet potato, peppers, eggplant, carrots, and onion with 3 tablespoon oil in a Dutch oven for 5 minutes. Separately sauté the garlic, turmeric,

cinnamon, curry powder, black pepper, and salt in a saucepan with 3 tablespoon oil for 3 minutes. Transfer this spiced oil to the Dutch oven and mix well. Stir in the almonds, garbanzo beans, orange juice, zucchini, and raisins; cover to cook for 20 minutes on a simmer. Stir in the spinach, cook for 5 minutes, and then serve warm.

Moroccan Lamb Kabobs

Preparation time: 10 minutes
Cook time: 16 minutes
Nutrition facts (per serving): 379 cal (11g fat, 34g protein, 3g fiber)

Moroccan lamb kabobs cooked with goat cheese is a fancy meal to serve for special dinners. These kabobs are cooked with mayonnaise and herbs to make the best blend of flavors.

Ingredients (6 servings)
2 pounds ground lamb
1 cup raisins
5 ounces goat cheese
⅓ cup mayonnaise
1 red onion, chopped
2 garlic cloves, chopped
2 tablespoons chopped fresh cilantro
¾ tablespoon ground cayenne pepper
½ teaspoon ground cumin
½ teaspoon ground coriander
Salt to taste
Coarsely ground black pepper to taste

Preparation
Preheat and prepare an outdoor grill on high heat. Grease its grates with oil. Mix the lamb meat with all the ingredients in a suitable mixing bowl. Divide the lamb meat mixture into 6 portions and wrap each portion around a skewer with wet hands. Grill the prepared skewers for 4 minutes per side. Serve warm.

Desserts

Moroccan Meskouta Orange Cake

Preparation time: 15 minutes
Cook time: 40 minutes
Nutrition facts (per serving): 347 cal (5g fat, 7g protein, 5g fiber)

A dessert that has no parallel, the Moroccan Meskouta orange cake is made with a zest orange-flavored batter.

Ingredients (8 servings)
1/2 cup (120 ml) orange juice
Zest of 2 oranges
4 large eggs
1 1/2 cups (300 grams) sugar
1/2 cup (120 ml) vegetable oil
2 cups (250 grams) flour
4 teaspoons baking powder
1/2 teaspoon salt
1 teaspoon vanilla

Preparation
At 350 degrees F, preheat your oven. Grease and flour a loaf pan. Beat the eggs with sugar in a bowl with an electric beater until thick. Stir in oil and mix well. Stir in salt, flour, and baking powder then mix well. Stir in orange juice, zest, and vanilla then mix well. Pour this orange cake batter in the loaf pan and bake for 40 minutes in the oven. Allow the cake to cool. Slice and serve.

Snake Cake (M'hanncha)

Preparation time: 15 minutes
Cook time: 20 minutes
Nutrition facts (per serving): 221 cal (3 g fat, 4 g protein, 2.8g fiber)

Yes, you can make something as delicious as these M'hanncha snacks by using only basic dessert and cake via some simple techniques.

Ingredients (12 servings)
Orange-Almond Paste
3 cups almonds
3/4 cup confectioners' sugar
1/2 teaspoon ground cinnamon
1/4 teaspoon ground cardamom
3/4 cup (1 ½ sticks) butter, melted
2 egg yolks, beaten
1 tablespoon orange-flower water
1 tablespoon orange juice
1 tablespoon grated orange zest
1 teaspoon vanilla extract

Assembly
12 (12 x 17-inch) sheets phyllo dough
3/4 cup (1 ½ sticks) butter, melted
2 egg yolks, beaten
1 tablespoon water
1/2 teaspoon cinnamon

Toppings
1/4 cup confectioners' sugar
4 teaspoons ground cinnamon
1/4 cup sliced almonds

Preparation

Mix the almonds with cinnamon, sugar, and cardamom in a food processor and blend into a coarse meal. Add the egg yolks and butter; then pulse until blended. Transfer this paste to a bowl and then add orange-flower water, orange zest, orange juice, and vanilla. Divide this paste into 12 balls, and refrigerate them for 30 minutes. Place these balls on a working surface, dusted with sugar. Roll each ball into 3 ½ inches long and refrigerate again for 30 minutes. At 350 degrees F, preheat your oven. Grease a suitable baking sheet with butter, spread a phyllo sheet on a working surface, and fold it into 4x17 inches rectangle. Brush the rectangle with melted butter. Repeat the same steps with four more phyllo sheets. Place one piece of the almond paste at one end of each rectangle sheet, and then roll to get a cylinder. Seal the edges of the roll with melted butter. Arrange these rolls in a coil shape, with their seam side down in a baking pan. Make more rolls to complete the coil. Beat the egg yolks with cinnamon and water in a bowl and brush over the cake. Bake for 20 minutes then allows it to cool. Mix the sugar with cinnamon and drizzle over the cake. Garnish with almonds. Serve.

Ghoriba Bahla

Preparation time: 15 minutes
Cook time: 41 minutes
Nutrition facts (per serving): 321 cal (8g fat, 4g protein, 1.4g fiber)

Try this *Ghoriba Bahla* on the menu. The sweet combination of almonds and sesame seeds are bliss for a sweet tooth like me.

Ingredients (12 servings)
2/3 cup granulated sugar
1/2 cup butter
1/2 cup vegetable oil
1/4 cup sesame seeds, toasted
1/4 cup blanched almonds, toasted and ground
1 teaspoon vanilla
1/8 teaspoon salt
4 cups flour
1 1/2 teaspoons baking powder

Preparation
At 400 degrees F, preheat your oven. Spread all the sesame seeds in a baking sheet and roast for 10 minutes. Transfer to a plate and add the almonds to the baking sheet and roast for 20 minutes at 350 degrees F. Grind the toasted almonds in a food processor. Mix the ground almond with sesame seeds, oil, butter, and sugar in a mixing bowl. Stir in half of the flour and baking powder and then mix well. Add the remaining flour and mix with hands. Knead the dough for 20 minutes. Roll the prepared dough into a smooth ball and then rub with oil. At 338 degrees F, preheat your oven. Layer a baking sheet with parchment paper. Divide the dough into 1 ½ inch balls and flatten them into a round disc. Place the dough disc in the prepared pan and broil for 6 minutes in the broiler. Then bake for almost 15 minutes in the oven. Serve.

Kaab el Ghazal

Preparation time: 10 minutes
Cook time: 12 minutes
Nutrition facts (per serving): 217 cal (17g fat, 5g protein, 0.8g fiber)

These *Kaab el ghazal* cookies will leave you spellbound due to their mildly sweet taste and the sensational almond fillings.

Ingredients (8 servings)
Almond Paste
1-pound (500 grams) almonds, blanched and peeled
1 1/3 cups (275 grams) sugar
1/3 cup (75 ml) orange flower water
1/4 cup (60 grams) butter
1/4 teaspoon cinnamon
1 pinch of mastic

Pastry Dough
3 cups (375 grams) flour
1/2 teaspoon salt
2 small eggs
3/4 cup (170ml) butter
4 tablespoons orange flower water

Egg Wash
1 egg
1 tablespoon orange flower water

Preparation
Grind the blanched almonds in a processor. Add cinnamon, sugar, gum, Arabic orange flour, and water then mix to make a paste. Make finger-length sticks out of this paste. Keep them aside, covered. Mix all the pastry dough ingredients in

a bowl and then knead for 20 minutes. Divide the dough into 4 portions, cover them with a plastic wrap, and leave for 15 minutes. Spread the dough portions into thin rectangles and place one almond stick on top of each. Pinch the edges together lengthwise. Place the cookies in a baking sheet. At 350 degrees F, preheat the oven. Beat the egg with 1 tablespoon orange flower water in a bowl. Brush the wash over the cookies and bake them for 12 minutes until golden.

Date Oatmeal Bars

Preparation time: 10 minutes
Cook time: 40 minutes
Nutrition facts (per serving): 308 cal (6g fat, 4g protein, 4g fiber)

The classic Moroccan flavors are on the menu, and this time, you can savor them through the date oatmeal bars.

Ingredients (16 servings)
Date Filling
3 cups dates, pitted and chopped
1 1/2 cups water
1/4 cup granulated sugar

Bars
1 cup packed brown sugar
1 cup butter or margarine softened
1 3/4 cups all-purpose
1 1/2 cups quick-cooking oats
1/2 teaspoon baking soda
1/2 teaspoon salt

Preparation
Mix all the filling ingredients in a cooking pan, cook for 10 minutes on low heat, and then allow the filling to cool for 5 minutes. At 400 degrees F, preheat your oven. Grease a 13 x9 inches baking pan with shortening. Mix brown sugar with butter in a large bowl. Stir in baking soda, oats, salt, and flour. Spread half of this mixture in the pan and top it with the filling mixture. Spread the remaining flour mixture on top and bake for 30 minutes. Allow it to cool, cut into 6 x 6 rows, and serve.

Moroccan Passover Haroset

Preparation time: 15 minutes
Nutrition facts (per serving): 169 cal (12g fat, 8g protein, 4g fiber)

The famous Moroccan Passover *Haroset* is essential to try on the Moroccan dessert menu. Bake at home with these healthy ingredients and enjoy!

Ingredients (8 servings)
2 cups pitted dates
1/2 cup golden raisins
1/2 cup dark raisins
1/2 cup walnuts
1-2 tablespoons sweet red Passover wine

Preparation
Blend all the dates, raisins, walnuts, and Passover wine in a food processor until it makes a crumbly paste. Make small walnuts sized balls from this mixture. Place them on a baking sheet and refrigerate for 1 hour. Serve.

Moroccan Stuffed Dates

Preparation time: 10 minutes
Nutrition facts (per serving): 202 cal (7g fat, 6g protein, 1.3g fiber)

If you're a stuffed date lover, then this Moroccan dessert recipe is the right fit for you. Try this at home and cook in no time.

Ingredients (6 servings)
1-pound (500 grams) dates
1 cup (150 grams) of almonds, blanched and peeled
1/4 cup (60 grams) sugar
1 1/2 tablespoons orange flower water
1 tablespoon butter
1/4 teaspoon cinnamon

Optional
a few drops food color
Granulated sugar
Walnut pieces

Preparation
Blend the sugar, blanched almonds, and cinnamon in a food processor. Add orange flower water, and butter. Next, blend until it makes a smooth paste. Add a few drops of food color, if desired, and mix well. Make cylinders from this paste, small enough to fit the dates. Take one date at a time and cut a vertical slit on top, remove its pit, and stuff it with one cylinder of almond paste. Stuff the remaining dates in the same way. Garnish with shredded coconut, cinnamon, and walnut. Drizzle sugar on top. Serve.

Moroccan Yogurt Cake

Preparation time: 10 minutes
Cook time: 45 minutes
Nutrition facts (per serving): 293 cal (18g g fat, 9g protein, 3g fiber)

The famous yogurt cake is another special dessert to try on the Moroccan menu. Try baking it at home with these healthy ingredients and enjoy it.

Ingredients (8 servings)
3 large eggs
1 small container plain yogurt
½ cup vegetable oil
1 cup sugar
1 ½ cups flour
4 teaspoons baking powder
1/2 teaspoon salt
2 teaspoons vanilla

Preparation
At 350 degrees F, preheat your oven. Grease a suitable Bundt pan with oil and dust it with flour. Beat the egg whites in a bowl with an electric mixer until fluffy. Beat the yogurt with egg yolks, sugar, and oil in another bowl. Stir in the flour, 4 teaspoons baking powder, salt, and vanilla; then mix well until smooth. Fold in the egg whites and mix gently. Spread the batter in the Bundt pan and bake for 45 minutes. Allow the cake to cool then serve.

Moroccan date cookies

Preparation time: 15 minutes
Cook time: 20 minutes
Nutrition facts (per serving): 201 cal (6g fat, 4g protein, 0.6g fiber)

A dessert that has no parallel, these date cookies have a delicious blend of dates and cookie dough that's baked and served.

Ingredients (8 servings)

For the Cookie Dough
4½ cups all-purpose flour
1 teaspoon baking powder
1 cup boiling water
9 ounces (250 grams) margarine
½ cup of vegetable oil
1 teaspoon vanilla extract

For the filling
12 ounces (350 grams) pitted dates
1 teaspoon cinnamon
4 tablespoon hot water (or as needed)

Preparation

Mix all the cookie dough ingredients in a suitable bowl to make a soft dough. Cover and keep it aside. Blend the pitted dates, ½ teaspoon cinnamon, and water in a food processor. At 350 degrees F, preheat your oven. Layer a cookie sheet with parchment paper. Place a spoonful of dough on your hand palm, spread it, and top it with 1 teaspoon filling, then wrap the dough around the filling. Place it on the baking sheet and continue making more cookies in this way. Bake these cookies for 20 minutes. Allow them to cool and then garnish with sugar and cinnamon. Enjoy.

Almond and Chocolate Ghriba

Preparation time: 10 minutes
Cook time: 13 minutes
Nutrition facts (per serving): 203 cal (7g fat, 3g protein, 1g fiber)

The Moroccan almond and chocolate Ghriba are great to serve with all the hot beverages, and they're popular for their prominent chocolaty taste.

Ingredients (21 servings)
7 1/2 ounces (200 grams) chocolate, 70% cocoa
1 2/3 ounces (50 grams) unsalted butter, softened
3 1/2 ounces (100 grams) caster sugar
2 eggs
1 teaspoon vanilla extract
½ teaspoon almond extract
5 ounces (150 grams) almond powder
3 1/2 ounces (100 grams) plain flour
1 heaped teaspoon baking powder
½ teaspoon salt
5 ounces (150 grams) icing sugar to coat the cookies

Preparation
Mix chocolate and the butter in a suitable bowl and heat in the microwave until melted. Stir in the sugar, eggs, vanilla, and almond extract. Mix these ingredients well until smooth. Add plain flour, almond flour, baking powder, and salt then mix all the ingredients together. Cover the mixture with a cling sheet and refrigerate for 2 hours. At 350 degrees F, preheat your oven. Take about 2 tablespoons of the prepared dough and make a ball from it. Roll each ball in icing sugar to coat well. Transfer the Ghriba cookies on a lined baking tray and press each ball into a cookie. Bake the cookies 13 minutes, until cracked on the outside. Allow them to cool for 15 minutes approximately and then serve.

Moroccan Milk Pastilla (Ktefa)

Preparation time: 10 minutes
Cook time: 10 minutes
Nutrition facts (per serving): 174 cal (14g fat, 7g protein, 2g fiber)

These Moroccan *Ktefa* are worth the try as they taste so unique and exotic. This dessert is definitely a must on the Moroccan menu.

Ingredients (6 servings)
10 sheets filo dough
5 oz. almonds blanched
2 cups of milk
3 tablespoon cornstarch
1/2 cup sugar
3 cups oil for frying
1/2 teaspoon vanilla
1 egg yolk

Preparation
Toast the almonds in a pan until golden, then grind them with 1 tablespoon sugar in a food processor. Cut all the filo sheets into two halves and deep fry them until golden. Next, transfer to a suitable plate lined with a paper towel. Beat the egg yolk with milk and cornstarch in a saucepan. Place it over medium heat and add sugar. Stir and cook the sauce until it thickens. In a platter, place 3 filo sheets and drizzle half of the almond on top and then add the remaining filo sheets on top. Finally, drizzle the remaining almonds on top and pour the milk sauce on top. Serve.

Moroccan Chocolate Cake

Preparation time: 15 minutes
Cook time: 40 minutes
Nutrition facts (per serving): 231 cal (6g fat, 4g protein, 2g fiber)

Without this chocolate cake, the Moroccan dessert menu is incomplete. Try them with different variations of toppings like chocolate syrup.

Ingredients (6 servings)
4 eggs
1 3/4 cups sugar
1 cup of vegetable oil
2 cups flour
3/4 cup unsweetened cocoa powder
4 teaspoons baking powder
1 teaspoon salt
1 1/4 cups milk or water
2 teaspoon vanilla

Preparation
At 350 degrees F, preheat your oven. Grease a 9 x 12 inches rectangular pan and dust with flour. Beat the eggs with oil and sugar in a bowl until creamy. Stir in the flour, baking powder, milk, salt, vanilla, and cocoa powder, and then beat for 2 minutes. Spread this batter in a rectangular pan and bake for 40 minutes, then allow it to cool then serve.

Seffa

Preparation time: 15 minutes
Cook time: 35 minutes
Nutrition facts (per serving): 149 cal (10g fat, 4g protein, 0g fiber)

The famous *Seffa* is essential to try on the Moroccan dessert menu. Try baking it at home with these healthy ingredients and enjoy it.

Ingredients (6 servings)
17 1/2 ounces (500 grams) of noodles
3 ounces (80 grams) raisins
3 1/2 ounces (100 grams) icing sugar
3 ounces (80 grams) of butter
3 1/2 ounces (100 grams) roasted almonds
1/4 tablespoon of oil
1 tablespoon of cinnamon
1 teaspoon salt

Preparation
Add enough water to fill half of a steaming pot and set it over medium heat. Place the noodles in the steamer, cover, and let it steam for 15 minutes. Mix noodles with 1/3 cup salted water and returned to the steamer and cook for 10 minutes. Then transfer to a plate and mix with 3 tablespoon of water. Return to the steamer and add raisins. Continue steaming for 10 minutes. Mix these noodles with butter and all the remaining ingredients in a bowl. Serve.

Moroccan Oranges with Orange Flower Water

Preparation time: 15 minutes
Cook time: 10 minutes
Nutrition facts (per serving): 115 cal (3g fat, 11g protein, 3g fiber)

Moroccan oranges are one good option in the desserts. You can also keep them ready and stored and use instead of cookies.

Ingredients (4 servings)
2 sweet oranges
2 to 4 tablespoon orange juice
1 tablespoon orange blossom water
1 teaspoon sugar
1/4 teaspoon ground cinnamon

For garnishing
1 pinch ground cinnamon

Preparation
Peel and slice the oranges horizontally into ¼ inch thick slices. Toss the remaining ingredients in a small bowl. Place the slices on a plate and drizzle the cinnamon mixture on top. Cover them with a cling film and refrigerate for 1 hour. Serve.

Moroccan Coconut Snowball Cookies

Preparation time: 10 minutes
Cook time: 20 minutes
Nutrition facts (per serving): 186 cal (12g fat, 4g protein, 2.5g fiber)

These coconut snowball cookies bring the Moroccan dessert menu to life. Try them with different variations of toppings.

Ingredients (12 servings)
3 eggs
1 cup (236 ml) vegetable oil
1 cup (200 grams) granulated sugar
1 teaspoon vanilla
3 1/4 cups (400 grams) flour
2 teaspoons baking powder
2 1/2 cups (625 grams) apricot jam
3 tablespoons orange flower water
2 1/2 cups (200 grams) grated desiccated coconut

Preparation
At 360 degrees F, preheat your oven. Layer two baking sheets with parchment paper. Beat the eggs with sugar, vanilla, and oil in a bowl until smooth. Stir in remaining ingredients and mix well. Divide the snowball cookie dough into small balls and place them in the baking sheet and press them in a cookie. Bake for 12 minutes approximately in the oven until golden. Allow them to cool. Add apricot jam and orange flower water to a saucepan, place it over medium heat, and cook until it makes a syrup. Dip the snowball cookies in the syrup and then coat them with coconut. Place the cookies on a baking sheet with parchment paper. Serve.

Halwa Dyal Makina

Preparation time: 10 minutes
Cook time: 16 minutes
Nutrition facts (per serving): 161 cal (4g fat, 2g protein, 1.1g fiber)

Here comes a dessert that's most loved by all. The *Halwa Dyal Makina* isn't only served as a dessert, but it's also famous street food.

Ingredients (12 servings)
3 large eggs
2/3 cup sugar
1/2 cup vegetable oil
1 teaspoon vanilla
Pinch of salt
1 cup of corn flour
3 cups flour
5 1/4 ounces dark chocolate

Preparation
Beat the eggs with oil and sugar in a mixer. Stir in vanilla, salt, and corn flour then mix until smooth. Add the flour and the mix until it makes a dough. Layer two baking trays with parchment paper. Add the prepared dough to a pastry bag with a fluted tip and pipe the dough into 2-inch strips onto the prepared baking sheets. At 350 degrees F, preheat your oven. Bake the Makina cookies for 15 minutes in the oven. Meanwhile, melt the chocolate in a bowl by heating in the microwave. Dip the ends of the *Makina* biscuits in the melted chocolate. Allow the cookies to cool and serve.

Drinks

Moroccan Avocado Almond Smoothie

Preparation time: 5 minutes
Nutrition facts (per serving): 112 cal (2g fat, 4 protein, 3g fiber)

Here comes a refreshing mix of avocado and almond in a nutritious smoothie. This drink is great to beat the heat of summers, and it's rich in antioxidants as well.

Ingredients (1 serving)
1/2 ripe Hass avocado, peeled and pitted
1 cup almond milk
1 teaspoon sugar

Preparation
Add all the cocktail ingredients to a blender and blend well for 30 seconds. Serve chilled.

Moroccan Mint White Chocolate Cocktail

Preparation time: 5 minutes
Nutrition facts (per serving): 163cal (7g fat, 3g protein, 1g fiber)

The Moroccan mint white chocolate cocktail is loved by all due to its refreshing taste and cool flavors. It's rich in energy and nutrients.

Ingredients (2 servings)
1 cup coconut cream
1/2 cup coconut milk
1/4 cup white chocolate
1 teaspoon mint extract
3-5 drops of green food coloring

Preparation
Add all the cocktail ingredients to a blender and blend well for 30 seconds. Serve chilled.

Moroccopolitan

Preparation time: 10 minutes
Nutrition facts (per serving): 117 cal (0g fat, 0g protein, 0g fiber)

The Moroccan drink is great to serve on all the special occasions and dinner. It has this appealing honey-mixed vodka taste.

Ingredients (2 servings)
4 drops Moroccan bitters
¼ cup pomegranate-infused vodka
1 ½ tablespoon honey syrup
1 tablespoon lemon juice

Preparation
Add all the cocktail ingredients to a suitable cocktail shaker and shake well for 30 seconds. Serve chilled.

Moroccan Almond Milkshake

Preparation time: 10 minutes
Nutrition facts (per serving): 142 cal (3g fat, 6.3g protein, 1g fiber)

The Moroccan almond milkshake is famous for its blend of blanched almonds with blossom water. You can prepare this drink easily at home.

Ingredients (6 servings)
1 cup blanched almonds
6 cups water
1/2 cup refined sugar
1 teaspoon orange blossom water

Preparation
Add all the cocktail ingredients to a blender and blend well for 30 seconds. Serve chilled.

Moroccotini

Preparation time: 5 minutes
Nutrition facts (per serving): 156 cal (0g fat, 0.7g protein, 1.4g fiber)

The Moroccotini is all that you need to celebrate the holidays. Keep the drink ready in your refrigerator for quick serving.

Ingredients (1 serving)
7 tablespoons orange-flavored vodka
1 tablespoon lime juice
2 tablespoons syrup
5 mint leaves

Preparation
Add all the cocktail ingredients to a suitable cocktail shaker and shake well for 30 seconds. Serve chilled.

Marrakech Mule

Preparation time: 5 minutes
Nutrition facts (per serving): 110 cal (0g fat, 0g protein, 2.3g fiber)

It's a special Moroccan mule drink, which is great to serve at special dinners and festive celebrations.

Ingredients (2 servings)
3 oz. tea Marrakesh mint
1 oz. el dorado silver rum
½ oz. Domaine de canton ginger liqueur
½ oz. Chambord

Preparation
Add all the cocktail ingredients to a suitable cocktail shaker and shake well for 30 seconds. Serve chilled.

If you liked Moroccan recipes, discover to how cook DELICIOUS recipes from Balkan countries!

Within these pages, you'll learn 35 authentic recipes from a Balkan cook. These aren't ordinary recipes you'd find on the Internet, but recipes that were closely guarded by our Balkan mothers and passed down from generation to generation.

Main Dishes, Appetizers, and Desserts included!

If you want to learn how to make Croatian green peas stew, and 32 other authentic Balkan recipes, then start with our book!

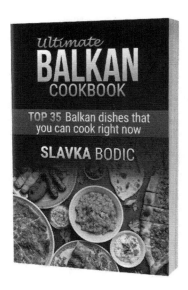

Order at www.balkanfood.org/cook-books now for only $2,99

If you're a Mediterranean dieter who wants to know the secrets of the Mediterranean diet, dieting, and cooking, then you're about to discover how to master cooking meals on a Mediterranean diet right now!

In fact, if you want to know how to make Mediterranean food, then this new e-book - "The 30-minute Mediterranean diet" - gives you the answers to many important questions and challenges every Mediterranean dieter faces, including:

- How can I succeed with a Mediterranean diet?
- What kind of recipes can I make?
- What are the key principles to this type of diet?
- What are the suggested weekly menus for this diet?
- Are there any cheat items I can make?

... and more!

If you're serious about cooking meals on a Mediterranean diet and you really want to know how to make Mediterranean food, then you need to grab a copy of "The 30-minute Mediterranean diet" right now.
Prepare **111 recipes with several ingredients in less than 30 minutes**!

Order at www.balkanfood.org/cook-books for only $2,99!

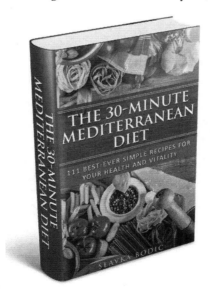

What could be better than a home-cooked meal? Maybe only a Greek homemade meal.

Do not get discouraged if you have no Greek roots or friends. Now you can make a Greek food feast in your kitchen.

This ultimate Greek cookbook offers you 111 best dishes of this cuisine! From more famous gyros to more exotic *Kota Kapama* this cookbook keeps it easy and affordable.

All the ingredients necessary are wholesome and widely accessible.
The author's picks are as flavorful as they are healthy. The dishes described in this cookbook are "what Greek mothers have made for decades."

Full of well-balanced and nutritious meals, this handy cookbook includes many vegan options. Discover a plethora of benefits of Mediterranean cuisine, and you may fall in love with cooking at home.

Inspired by a real food lover, this collection of delicious recipes will taste buds utterly satisfied.

Order at www.balkanfood.org/cook-books for only $2,99!

Maybe to try exotic Syrian cuisine?

From succulent *sarma*, soups, warm and cold salads to delectable desserts, the plethora of flavors will satisfy the most jaded foodie. Have a taste of a new culture with this **traditional Serbian cookbook**.

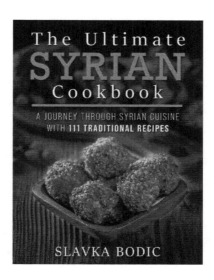

Order at www.balkanfood.org/cook-books for only $2,99!

ONE LAST THING

If you enjoyed this book or found it useful, I'd be very grateful if you could find the time to post a short review on Amazon. Your support really does make a difference and I read all the reviews personally, so I can get your feedback and make this book even better.

Thanks again for your support!

Please send me your feedback at:

www.balkanfood.org

Printed in Great Britain
by Amazon

35762763R00095